NINE GLORIOUS MONTHS

Also by Michelle Leclaire O'Neill

Creative Childbirth: The Complete Leclaire Method

NINE *Glorious* MONTHS

Daily Meditations and Reflections
for Your Pregnancy

MICHELLE LECLAIRE O'NEILL

PRIMA PUBLISHING

PRIMA PUBLISHING and colophon are registered trademarks of Prima Communications, Inc.

ISBN 0-7615-0795-7

96 97 98 99 00 AA 10 9 8 7 6 5 4 3 2 1
Printed in the United States of America

How to Order:
Single copies may be ordered from Prima Publishing, P.O. Box 1260BK, Rocklin, CA 95677; telephone (916) 632-4400. Quantity discounts are also available. On your letterhead, include information concerning the intended use of the books and the number of books you wish to purchase.

Visit us online at http://www.primapublishing.com

For my children:

Brendan

Erin

Maria

My deepest thanks and appreciation to Ruth Giron-Redmond for her delightful and even temperament and for her wonderful expertise in word processing and the deciphering of my handwriting of this book, even into her fortieth week of pregnancy.

Thanks to all the pregnant mothers and fathers who shared their thoughts, feelings, pregnancies, labors, and births with me.

NINE GLORIOUS MONTHS

1st Month

Suddenly, as if without a reason,

   Heart, Brain and Body and Imagination

   All gather in tumultuous joy together

Harold Munro

Sunday

In the Broad Daylight
Thou art unseen, but yet I
hear thy shrill delight

Percy Bysshe Shelley

Today I begin to imagine you. Your backbone is forming. Some of your vertebrae are in place. I hope I am able to give you the emotional support to continue to develop and to one day stand up for what you believe in.

Today my heightened awareness is:

Today's reawakening is:

Today's note to my baby:

Monday

Your brain is more developed now. You are a living being within me. I shall relax as much as I can and send soothing messages to your developing brain. I rejoice in the miracle that you are.

Joyous and clear and

fresh—thy music

doth surpass

Percy Bysshe Shelley

Today my concern is:

Today I acknowledge:

Today's note to my baby:

Tuesday

Teach us, sprite or bird

What sweet thoughts

   are thine:

I have never heard

Praise of love or wine

That panted forth a

   flood of rapture

   so divine

Percy Bysshe Shelley

Your spinal cord is more developed. My body is a sacred vessel. It is caring for the wonder of you within me. I'm taking prenatal vitamins and I'm relaxing daily for at least twenty minutes so that I can foster a nurturing environment in which you can grow.

Today I want to avoid:

Today I want to address:

Today's note to my baby:

Wednesday

It's difficult at times to grasp the reality of you within me. Your nervous system is more developed. You are a sensate being. I must take care of what I think. My thoughts become feelings that I send to you. I need to change my negative thinking patterns so you can have peaceful floatings.

Today's vulnerability is:

Today my purpose is:

Today's note to my baby:

Teach me half the
gladness
That thy brain must
know;
Such harmonious
madness
From my lips would
flow,
The world should
listen then as I am
listening now.

Percy Bysshe Shelley

Thursday

We shall by morning
Inherit the earth.
Our foot's in the door.

Sylvia Plath

You now have buds for your arms and legs. I visualize them forming and wish them well in their growth. One day, I'll kiss your tiny toes and feet; you'll grasp my finger, and I'll let you hold on for as long as you want.

Today my need is:

Today my intuition is:

Today's note to my baby:

Friday

You have two folds of tissue that will grow to be your sweet ears. May you hear the sounds of love, equality, peace, serenity, and joy. The magical convolutions of your ears are taking place inside of me. I am in awe.

*Music I hear with you
is more than music
And bread I break
with you is more
than bread.*

Conrad Aiken

Today my resistance is:

Today my aspirations are:

Today's note to my baby:

Saturday

That's the wise thrush;

  he sings each song twice
  over

Lest you should think he

  never could recapture

That first fine careless

  rapture.

Robert Browning

The lenses of your eyes are now appearing. You're getting so many wondrous gifts in such a short period of time, and I bet you're accepting them with ease. I wish I could say the same. Sometimes I feel a bit anxious about being a parent. Why, I haven't even come to terms yet with being a daughter and a partner! Maybe I can learn from you and grow and develop in new ways along with you. Perhaps I need to see through new lenses in my own eyes. Perhaps I ought to look differently at some things.

Today my limitations are:

Today my desire is:

Today's note to my baby:

Sunday

Now you're about one-quarter of an inch long: an embryo. When I look at a ruler and what one-quarter of an inch is, it is hard to imagine your form, your size, and all that you already are. I still can't grasp the reality of you and motherhood and pregnancy. I'm trying. The best that I can do now is eat a healthy diet, exercise gently, and continue my daily twenty-minute relaxation. Today I think I'll focus on the perfect you, who you already are, and how you can fit on my thumbnail. You amaze me.

Today my denial is:

Today I am grateful for:

Today's note to my baby:

This carol they began that hour,
With a hey, and a ho and a hey nonino,
How that a life is but a flower.
In the spring time, the only pretty ring time.
When birds do sing hey ding a ding, ding!
Sweet lovers love the spring.

And therefore take the present time,
with a hey and a ho and a hey nonino.

William Shakespeare

Monday

Oh, thou art fairer than the evening air.
Clad in the beauty of a thousand stars;
Brighter art thou than flaming Jupiter
More lovely than the monarch of the sky.

Christopher Marlowe

Your brain is growing rapidly and your backbone is now shaped. I send curiosity and wonder to your forming brain, and I send the strength of your convictions to your backbone. May you find it easy to be all of who you are.

Today my heightened awareness is:

Today's reawakening is:

Today's note to my baby:

Tuesday

Your mouth is a closed one now, and I know that there are dark hollows where your eyes and ears will eventually be—may these be the only dark hollows you ever have. I wish you a mouth that feels as comfortable closed as open; I wish you the wisdom to know when one is better than the other. I blow a kiss into your accepting hollows.

Today my concern is:

Today I acknowledge:

Today's note to my baby:

And I will make thee beds
  of roses,
And a thousand fragrant
  posies,
A cup of flowers and
  a kirtle
Embroidered all with
  leaves of myrtle

Christopher Marlowe

Wednesday

I am the darker brother.

They send me to eat in the

kitchen

When company comes,

But I laugh

And eat well

And grow strong.

Langston Hughes

Your digestive tract is developing. May you be able to assimilate all that is important and to digest that which is life-enhancing—and may you learn how to disregard the rest. Today I let go of all that is not advantageous to your growth and development.

Today I want to avoid:

Today I want to address:

Today's note to my baby:

Thursday

The germ cells that will form into your ovaries or testes are there within you. Whatever sex you are, may your path be one of peace and nurturance. May you be strong and gentle, discriminating and accepting, rational and intuitive. Today I surrender to the moment. I am free of the past and the future. I am exalted by the now.

Today's vulnerability is:

Today my purpose is:

Today's note to my baby:

Freedom

Is a strong seed

Planted

In a great need

I live here too

I want freedom

Just as you.

Langston Hughes

Friday

Tra la la! The birds are

chirruping!

Fields are green and

flowers are gay!

Ogden Nash

Your skeleton is present, but it is not etched in bone yet. May you always be flexible yet may you never waver from your truth. May you know how to find what your need deep within your soul (when does that form, at what moment?). Today I'll nurture your soul and mine. I'll meditate on the vastness of the sky and the distant light of the stars; on the brilliance of the sun and the clarity of a raindrop; on the color of a lilac and the sound of a cricket. I'll meditate on all of this and still not approximate the grandeur of your soul.

Today my need is:

Today my intuition is:

Today's note to my baby:

Saturday

I am told that there is a tail at the end of your spinal cord! A remnant, I guess, of our saurian tail. Only monkeys still parade with their tails: with great ease they move from place to place; with great delight they live, unless disturbed by technology. May you know before you act, and may you swing through your environment with the delight and enthusiasm of your ancestors. May your birth be as in the wild, without machines and bright lights. May you slip out into the baby catcher's hands, onto my belly, into my arms. Hail to the remnants of the past! You are free.

Today my resistance is:

Today my aspirations are:

Today's note to my baby:

The cow is of the bovine ilk;
One end is moo, the other milk.

Ogden Nash

Sunday

Let even obstetricians fall
   quiet,
For Chloë is on her latest
   diet
So rapidly our Chloë passes
From bananas to wheat
   germ and molasses.
First she will eat but chops
   and cheese
Next only things that grow
   in trees.

Ogden Nash

You have grown again. By the end of this week, you'll be one-half inch long. I'll help you this week in your big stretch. I'll eat lots of whole grains, miso soup, and all the leafy green vegetables I can. I'll eat various beans and a sea vegetable or two. This week my eating will be my meditation. I'll eat in silence at least one meal a day. I'll chew my food till it becomes liquid in my mouth, so you can receive all the nourishment and vitamins the food can provide you.

Today my limitations are:

Today my desire is:

Today's note to my baby:

Monday

Now your heart beats inside your chest. It is truly yours. Our heart rates are different, and yet, in many ways, I am responsible for the way yours beats. I will work on being calm. I'll exercise today. Perhaps I'll walk for twenty minutes and I'll start a routine of doing that with you daily. Walking will soothe me, and in becoming calm I'll be able to create a peaceful environment for you.

Today my denial is:

Today I am grateful for:

Today's note to my baby:

A golden bird was singing
its melody divine
I found you and I loved
you,
And all the world was
mine.

Paul Laurence Dunbar

Tuesday

Now buttermilk, now milk
 that's malted,
And saccharin and salt
 de-salted,
Lean fish and fowl as gaunt
 as avarice,
And haggard haggis and
 curds cadaverous

Ogden Nash

Now your stomach, your intestines, and your other organs are forming. It's important that I eat unprocessed foods. Sometimes that's difficult. This is another very important week of your development. I'll really concentrate on my diet so that I can nourish you properly. I see you developing a normal, healthy, and strong constitution. There is much food to choose from; I'll give you only the best.

Today my heightened awareness is:

Today's reawakening is:

Today's note to my baby:

Wednesday

Your sweet face is forming. This week it flattens, and you get little openings for your nose. Let's see, whose nose would I like you to have? Well, I guess it doesn't really matter as long as you can inhale and exhale easily through your nasal passages and as long as you can appreciate and differentiate smells. Today I'm going to have fun smelling all the different spices in the pantry. Maybe I'll even take you to the woods so I can send you the excitement of other scents. I can't wait to smell your brand-new baby smell.

Today my concern is:

Today I acknowledge:

Today's note to my baby:

The healthy crops of
*   whitening rice*
'Mongst thyme woods and
*   groves of spice,*
For adoration grow,
And marshaled in the
*   fencèd land,*
The peaches and
*   pomegranates stand*
Where wild carnations
*   blow.*

Christopher Smart

Thursday

To see a world in a grain of
sand
And a heaven in a wild
flower
Hold infinity in the palm of
your hand,
And eternity in an hour.

William Blake

This week you also begin to grow muscle fibers. Maybe you can even make micromovements. How interesting it must be to move a muscle for the first time. Today on my walk, I'll pay particular attention to my leg muscles. I'll become increasingly aware of each fiber as I walk, so I can share the newness with you. Happy growth spurts!

Today I want to avoid:

Today I want to address:

Today's note to my baby:

Friday

You are now a unique human. A special little embryonic person. I'm trying to make life for you as calm and as safe as I can. I'll be quiet with you and explore some ambivalent feelings of mine that may be assaulting you and preventing you from being perfectly comfortable. You make me aware of so many feelings that I usually just put aside. You experience the chemistry of my emotions, so I should be honest about them. There are some things from my family that I don't want to pass on to you and some things that I do. Let's discuss that a bit now, okay?

....

Today's vulnerability is:

....

Today my purpose is:

....

Today's note to my baby:

*The light was on the golden
  sands,
A glimmer on the sea;
My soul spoke clearly to
  thy soul,
Thy spirit answered me.*

Paul Laurence Dunbar

Saturday

Your clear eye is the one

absolutely beautiful

thing

I want to fill it with color

and ducks

The zoo of the new.

Sylvia Plath

Now your tail has almost disappeared. However, you must always remember from whence you came. That is very important, for someday someone may want you to be a Social Security number or a credit history, which has nothing to do with who you are. Your first home was out in the fresh air and in the trees. Never forget your origins, and you'll be able to find your own branch in the sky, your own place in the grass, your own footsteps on the floor of the forest. Keep the shadow of your tail and let it guide you to your own feast.

Today my need is:

Today my intuition is:

Today's note to my baby:

Sunday

Well, you are no longer an embryo, in case you're interested. You have now graduated to a fetus; by the end of this week, you'll be all of one inch long. You're quite an amazing creature for your size. You just keep moving right along, one step at a time. You're doing really well. I'm proud of your growth and development. We'll have a lovely day today to celebrate your new status. I'll take some deep breaths of fresh air and send them into my uterus, and I'll relax in whatever we do so that you can continue to feel safe and to grow inside of me.

Today my resistance is:

Today my aspirations are:

Today's note to my baby:

*We step like plush, we
   stand like snow,
The waters murmur now,
Three rivers and a hill
   are passed,
Two deserts and the sea.*

Sylvia Plath

Monday

The mountains grow
*   unnoticed,*
Their purple figures rise
Without attempt,
*   exhaustion*
Assistance or applause.

    Emily Dickinson

Now you have a jawline and your facial features are becoming more clear. You still don't look like the final you yet. Your face is as you are today. Although I can't see you, I can feel the surge of your presence within me.

Today my limitations are:

Today my desire is:

Today's note to my baby:

Tuesday

Your teeth are forming this week. One by one, they align above the smooth skin of your gums as your tooth buds secrete enamel and dentine; one day, they will break through your gums, and then you'll have twenty magnificent baby teeth. Your palate is also coming into being. I must eat exceptionally well so the two halves fuse together. You need a lot of calcium now so that your teeth grow white and your palate forms a perfect separation between your mouth and your nasal cavity. What a structure you are. Bit by bit, you're coming together.

Today my denial is:

Today I am grateful for:

Today's note to my baby:

Nature the gentlest mother,
Impatient of no child
The feeblest or the
*   waywardest*
Her admiration mild.

Emily Dickinson

Wednesday

Will there really be
*   a morning?*
Is there such a thing or day?
Could I see it from the
*   mountains*
If I were tall as they?

Emily Dickinson

Your arms are now long enough so that you can touch your own face. Your larynx has begun to develop. One day, you'll have a voice of your own. Today we'll celebrate. I'll sing a song that will be ours. I'll sing it to you every week until you are born. You'll know it well. When you reach my arms and I sing it once more, it will be like old times and you'll feel safe again, and one day when we're playing together in the bathtub we'll sing the song together and we'll remember.

Today my heightened awareness is:

Today's reawakening is:

Today's note to my baby:

Thursday

A lot is happening to you this week. Now you're not only a human being but a male or a female being. Unfortunately, in this world, that still makes a big difference. There are some laws about equality, and that's wonderful, but it's still difficult to follow your bliss if it's different from the cultural expectation. I hope you are delighted to be whatever sex you are.

Today my concern is:

Today I acknowledge:

Today's note to my baby:

There are words like
*   Freedom.*
Sweet and wonderful to say
On my heart string
*   freedom sings*
All day every day.

There are words like liberty
That almost make me cry
If you had known what I
*   knew*
You would know why.

Langston Hughes

Friday

Freedom

Is a strong seed

Planted

In a great need.

I live here too

I want freedom

Just as you.

Langston Hughes

I've been thinking about your sexual development. Societies everywhere differentiate so vehemently between boys and girls. I don't really understand why they have to define your growth and development. I'm glad I can protect you for a while longer. It's really hard to be a girl or a boy instead of a person. To me, you're a wondrous little being growing inside of me, and your feelings and your formation are all that matter to me.

Today I want to avoid:

Today I want to address:

Today's note to my baby:

Saturday

Your head is now about half your size. May you have your head on straight. And who shall decide what straight is and what thoughts and ideas should fill that amazing skull of yours? May your thinking be healthy, creative, and adventurous. And who is to say what your limits are and what your potential is?

I'm like that old mule
Black and—and don't give
  a damn!
You got to take me
Like I am.

Langston Hughes

Today's vulnerability is:

Today my purpose is:

Today's note to my baby:

Sunday

Invisible, visible, the world
Does not work without
both

Rumi

Well, fetus of mine, you've been here a while now. Your residence is quite established, and of that I am thrilled. I hope that I have been caring for you well. Sometimes I am overwhelmed by the thought of you. When I close my eyes and place my hands on my belly and feel the comfort of my own inhalations and exhalations—when I stay in this very moment, I feel safe and peaceful.

Today my need is:

Today my intuition is:

Today's note to my baby:

Monday

Our new organ together: our placenta. How efficient it is now, producing all the hormones that are necessary for your nurturance. It has a life of its own, manufacturing the estrogen that helps my uterus, your home, to grow and to develop new uterine blood vessels. A common language, a fluid poem we are: you and I. Such resonance. I listen to us together.

If you have a body, where is the spirit?
If you're spirit, what is the body?

Rumi

Today my resistance is:

Today my aspirations are:

Today's note to my baby:

Tuesday

The lenses, our bodily

personalities, seem

identical,

But the globe of soul fruit

We make

Each is elaborately

Unique

Rumi

The placenta through which you and I communicate is also now responsible for progesterone. That's a special hormone that prevents my uterus from contracting strongly until you've reached term. When you're ready to be born, when you're fully developed, then we'll let the level drop. Until then, it's you and I and our well-functioning organ. Let's have a cup of miso soup. Let's drink to our amazing placenta. Salud!

Today my limitations are:

Today my desire is:

Today's note to my baby:

Wednesday

Ah yes, the milk glands in my breasts are now developing so that I can feed you when you arrive. I can remember when I first began to develop breasts and even before then, when I wanted to have them develop, so I could look like a woman instead of a girl. Now I'm a bit ambivalent. I don't want to look like one big mammary gland. I close my eyes and remember, and I'm a little sad, a bit scared, and rather excited.

Today my denial is:

Today I am grateful for:

Today's note to my baby:

I walk into a huge pasture.
I nurse the milk of millennia

Rumi

Thursday

Remember when you drank

rain in the garden

Rumi

I'm still thinking about the milk ducts that are developing. My body is anticipating your arrival in this world, and you still have quite a long way to go. The feast is being prepared long ahead of your arrival. May my milk flow and may it be as nourishing to you as my uterus is.

Today my heightened awareness is:

Today's reawakening is:

Today's note to my baby:

Friday

Now you're drawing your food through your umbilical cord—your connection to the placenta. I once again close my eyes and this time imagine the sound of nourishment passing through to your grape-like weight.

You and I will be together

Till the universe dissolves

Rumi

Today my concern is:

Today I acknowledge:

Today's note to my baby:

Saturday

After a day or two,

lilies sprout,

The shape of my tongue

Rumi

My skin is a little softer now, and I even look a bit younger. Am I too young to be a mother or am I too old—or does age have anything to do with it? Maybe with each of your growth spurts and each hormonal fluctuation, I'll grow more and more naturally into motherhood. I accept the role. I accept you within me, and I accept my own bodily changes and my growth spurts. I know it's rather superficial, but I do hope I'll remain attractive.

Today I want to avoid:

Today I want to address:

Today's note to my baby:

Sunday

Now you are about one and three-quarter inches long, and your uterine home has expanded to the size of an orange. It's hard to imagine having a house that grows with all of your appendages. You and your house are still hidden deep within my pelvis. Enjoy your solitude. It can get hectic out here.

I'll never live again in
the limits of a lake
Next time the ocean!
I'll make the infinite
my home.

Rumi

Today's vulnerability is:

Today my purpose is:

Today's note to my baby:

Monday

My breasts are getting heavier. They are a good reminder of what is going on in my body. Sometimes I forget until I dress, and then I realize that I need a lot more support for my breasts. I really am manufacturing milk. How astounding!

Today my need is:

Today my intuition is:

Today's note to my baby:

While sweetly, gently

secretly,

The flowery bells of morn

are stirred

And the wise choirs

of faery

Begin (innumerous)

to be heard

James Joyce

Tuesday

Your ankles are now formed. May there be a strong connection between your feet and your legs so that you can travel well on your own. May you move lightly through life, and may your gait be easy, steady, and remarkable.

The odorous winds
are weaving
A music of sighs!
Arise, arise!
My dove, my beautiful one!

James Joyce

Today my resistance is:

Today my aspirations are:

Today's note to my baby:

Wednesday

When round his head the

aureole clings,

And he is clothed in white

I'll take his hand and go

with him

To the deep wells of light,

And into a stream we will

step down,

And bathe there

in God's sight.

Dante Gabriel Rossetti

Your wrists are formed. I circle them in my mind with ribbons and garlands of flowers. May your connection between your hands and your arms be ever so strong. May you reach out to the world with great wonder and joy, and may you receive all the gifts you are able to acknowledge. May you nurture and caress well. May you give freely and receive graciously.

Today my limitations are:

Today my desire is:

Today's note to my baby:

Thursday

My breasts are needing even more support now. I'll get them ready for you by massaging them daily. I'll rub sesame oil over my entire breast, paying special attention to my nipples. It's like setting the table for a wonderful feast.

Maples swell with sap
a-syruping!
Nature is spreading herself
today!

Ogden Nash

Today my denial is:

Today I am grateful for:

Today's note to my baby:

Friday

And your raised hands
gently touch the moon.

Vicente Aleixandre

Well, your fingers are clearly visible now. Five perfect fingers fluttering in sacred exhalations of touch. I open my palms and spread my fingers softly across my face. I cannot embrace your touch.

Today my heightened awareness is:

Today's reawakening is:

Today's note to my baby:

Saturday

Your toes also are now clearly identifiable: a silkworm's gentle spinning.
I stop all outward motion and feel the magnificence of my own breath. I
do not quite realize you.

Wild goose, wild goose,
At what age
Did you make your first

journey?

Issa

Today my concern is:

Today I acknowledge:

Today's note to my baby:

Sunday

O thou, Radiant

    Incorporeal

The I of earth and

    mankind, hurl

Down these seaboards

    across this continent,

The thousand-rayed discus

    of thy mind,

And above our walking

    limbs unfurl

Spirit torsos of exquisite

    Strength!

        Jean Toomer

Today I relax a bit. Your rate of growth slows down. I go about my life, always aware of your presence within me.

Today I want to avoid:

Today I want to address:

Today's note to my baby:

Monday

The amount of blood circulating throughout my body has begun to increase. I am filled with the energy of an emerging life force within me. Red and glowing, my being and yours are intensified.

And the pour of moonlight

swims over my body

Helen Wolfert

Today's vulnerability is:

Today my purpose is:

Today's note to my baby:

Tuesday

Today is a good time to start arranging childbirth classes so that I can share you and my thoughts of you with other mothers and fathers. We need to discuss all this. It's a time for sharing, not isolation.

My two breasts that were

fine and as

White as are mushrooms

Are now covered with

honey, and fingers

of moon

Have rounded them as with

the pulp of a fruit

Helen Wolfert

Today my need is:

Today my intuition is:

Today's note to my baby:

Wednesday

Now you have testicles or ovaries. Testicles: a sign of male strength and virility. Ovaries: the exaltation of fruit in female animals and in plants. I make no judgment. I have always had ovaries. Is it possible that I now have testicles within me too? Or do I have a whole new cascade of ovaries whirling within my womb?

When you begin,
  begin at the beginning.
Begin with the magic,
  begin with the sun,
Begin with the grass.

Helen Wolfert

Today my resistance is:

Today my aspirations are:

Today's note to my baby:

Thursday

Oh, darling,

let your body in

Let it tie you in,

In comfort.

Anne Sexton

The chambers of your heart are forming. May each one of them know love and understanding, rapture and harmony. Ah ohm, ah ohm, lub dub, lub dub . . . and we go on through eternity.

Today my limitations are:

Today my desire is:

Today's note to my baby:

Friday

Your red blood cells are now being produced by your liver and spleen. Radiant with the element of life, they march in honorable procession.

They dance to the lute
Two at a time

Anne Sexton

Today my denial is:

Today I am grateful for:

Today's note to my baby:

Saturday

We are strong
We are the good ones
Do not discover us
for we lie together
*   all in green*
like pond weeds.

Anne Sexton

Your white blood cells are being formed in your lymph nodes and in your thymus. Amazing cells that know exactly how to keep you free from all sorts of worldly poisons. Today we are responsive to all the healing exemptions from the sun, the sky, the air, the moon, the earth, and the stars. Today we are a single cord stretched between the heavens and the earth.

Today my heightened awareness is:

Today's reawakening is:

Today's note to my baby:

Sunday

Now you are about three inches long. I think of you as a leaf: translucent, illuminated, leaning toward the sun. Spirit and matter, unperceived and audible.

Each cell has a life
There is enough here
to please a nation

Anne Sexton

Today my concern is:

Today I acknowledge:

Today's note to my baby:

Monday

For this thing the body
   needs
Let me sing
For the supper
For the kissing
For the correct
Yes

            Anne Sexton

Your own greater intelligence already exists. You know how to defend against foreign intruders. You know what your body has to expel. I help to enhance your immune system by maintaining a steady, moderate exercise program; eating plenty of green leafy vegetables, yellow vegetables, and fruit; and taking my prenatal vitamins, including folic acid and iron.

Today I want to avoid:

Today I want to address:

Today's note to my baby:

Tuesday

Now your face is well developed. As I move my hands across my belly, I try to outline your visage. Your eyes are fused together; mine are gently closed in concentration of you. What will you look like? What will *you* see?

Today's vulnerability is:

Today my purpose is:

Today's note to my baby:

This great God.
Like a mammy bending
over her baby;
Kneeled down in the dust
Toiling over a lump of clay
Till he shaped it in his own
image

James Weldon Johnson

Wednesday

You can now move the muscles of your face to squint, and you can open and close your mouth. I scrunch my face tightly and open and close my mouth in fish-like movement trying to imagine you.

The glory of the day was
in her face,
The beauty of the night
was in her eyes.
All over her loveliness,
the grace
Of morning blushing in the
early skies

James Weldon Johnson

Today my need is:

Today my intuition is:

Today's note to my baby:

Thursday

This week, my uterus has risen above my pelvis. The doctor and/or midwife can feel it on external examination. Now we'll be checked at least once a month for quite a while. It's nice to be taken care of by people who know what's happening to us both.

And now unwittingly,
you've made me dream
Of violets, and my soul's
forgotten gleam.

Alice Dunbar Moore Nelson

Today my resistance is:

Today my aspirations are:

Today's note to my baby:

Friday

Beyond plants are animals
Beyond animals is man,
Beyond man is the
  universe.

The Big light
Let the Big Light in!

Jean Toomer

I know you are moving, making fists and kicking. I can't feel you yet. Soon, though, you'll be communicating to me with your arms and your legs, your hands and your feet, your elbows and your knees. I hope I am intuitive enough to understand your messages.

Today my limitations are:

Today my desire is:

Today's note to my baby:

Saturday

Now you probably swallow amniotic fluid frequently and absorb it into your bloodstream through your very own digestive tract. You then excrete some of it through your kidneys, taking in and absorbing what is desired and letting go of the rest. You're learning the process of life.

As I row over the plain
Of the sea and gaze
Into the distance, the waves
Merge with the bright sky.

Fujiwara No Tadamichi

....

Today my denial is:

....

Today I am grateful for:

....

Today's note to my baby:

Sunday

Send peace on all the lands
   and flickering Corn,
O, may tranquillity walk
   by his elbow
When wandering in the
   forest.

William Butler Yeats

Well, my sweet, we're in this together, you and I. I do hope you like the environment that I've created within my uterus, your home.

Today my heightened awareness is:

Today's reawakening is:

Today's note to my baby:

Monday

I understand that you have some control over your stay here and that your own support of yourself contributes to your well-being. I do hope that you are comfortable and content.

To and fro we leap
And chase the frothy
    bubbles,
While the world is full
    of troubles
And is anxious in its sleep.

William Butler Yeats

Today my concern is:

Today I acknowledge:

Today's note to my baby:

Tuesday

Now folds the lily all her
*   sweetness up,*
And slips into the bosom
*   of the lake.*
So fold thyself, my dearest,
*   thou, and slip*
Into my bosom and be lost
*   in me*

Alfred Tennyson

I know that I have a few daily worries: bills and nourishing you and gaining weight. These are minimum concerns, I understand. I know that you cannot take a continual assault of anxiety hormones, so I'll try to deal with things as they arise so they don't build up inordinately.

Today I want to avoid:

Today I want to address:

Today's note to my baby:

Wednesday

By dealing with issues as they arise, I try to set your emotional thermostat at a healthy level. I really want to do that for you. Is this possible? What a tremendous responsibility!

Deer walk upon our mountains, and the quail
Whistle about us their
*   spontaneous cries;*
Sweet berries ripen in the
*   wilderness.*

Wallace Stevens

....
Today's vulnerability is:

....
Today my purpose is:

....
Today's note to my baby:

Thursday

Your growth and development is much more subtle now. My behavior, however, needs to be explicit, as your physiology is so fine-tuned to my every move. Smoking can cut your oxygen supply. Alcohol can maim or even kill you. No wild nights—just sweet guitars and abstinence.

In the company of fair
young maids the
Spanish ale went round
'tis a bitter change from
those gay days that now
I'm forced to go.

George Fox

Today my need is:

Today my intuition is:

Today's note to my baby:

Friday

I know that you are very resilient. Occasionally I do ignore your physical needs. Sometimes I overeat and drink caffeine and don't rest enough. What you need is not unreasonable—I just find discipline difficult at times.

Today my resistance is:

Today my aspirations are:

Today's note to my baby:

*From a dark and
narrow street
Into a world of love.
A child was born,
speak low,
Speak reverent.*

Dora Greenwell

Saturday

When I acknowledge your psychological needs, I suppose I am also acknowledging my own. We both want love and attention. I know you like it when I rub my belly. Somehow you perceive my gentle touch.

One by one objects are

defined—

It quickens; clarity, outline

of leaf

But now the stark dignity

of entrance

William Carlos Williams

Today my limitations are:

Today my desire is:

Today's note to my baby:

Sunday

Perhaps you and Daddy and I should set a date for at least five minutes every day. Daddy and I will rub my belly and chat with you so you can enjoy a tranquil swim and feel protected and nurtured by us both.

Is there place in the land of
  your labour;
Is there room in your world
  of delight

Algernon Charles Swinburne

Today my denial is:

Today I am grateful for:

Today's note to my baby:

Monday

Revolving

blazing and meditating

before it halts at some final

point which consecrates it

Stéphane Mallarmé

Now you have clear patterns of movements. I can't feel you yet, though sometimes I think I have vague sensations of you, like a very distant star.

Today my heightened awareness is:

Today's reawakening is:

Today's note to my baby:

Tuesday

As I understand it, you also have established a resting rhythm. I'm not quite aware of that yet, either. I look forward to understanding your communications.

Today my concern is:

Today I acknowledge:

Today's note to my baby:

Flowers nodding gaily,
  scent in air,
Flowers posied,
  flowers for the hair,
Sleepy flowers, flowers
  bold to stare—O pick me
some!

Thomas Sturge Moore

Wednesday

Thou dost float and run,

Like an unbodied joy

whose race is just begun.

Percy Bysshe Shelley

I know that during this phase you are stretching and thrusting your arms and legs outward. What is that like, to move for the first time? I bet it's as gentle as a cloud floating across the sky.

Today I want to avoid:

Today I want to address:

Today's note to my baby:

Thursday

And so you continue to alternate movement with periods of quiet, motionless sleep. Like a soft breeze, you move inside me and then, like a quiet mist, you hush all about you.

*She knew this instant
 would remain
A sacrament not touched
 again.*

Robert Peter Tristram Coffin

Today's vulnerability is:

Today my purpose is:

Today's note to my baby:

Friday

The wind in the reeds
and the rushes,
The bees on the bells
of thyme,
The birds on the myrtle
bushes,
The circle above
in the lime.

Percy Bysshe Shelley

I recall a ring of mountains and a layer of whispering clouds hovering in their center, silently protecting all below. In that stillness was great peace. May you always keep a space inside you for that grand silence. It is the most important part of you.

Today my need is:

Today my intuition is:

Today's note to my baby:

Saturday

Soon you will rise up again—little tai chi movements, wondrous thrusts and stirrings—and I still am unable to really feel that it is you. I await a strong knock. I admit I am impatient when it comes to having a definite awareness of you.

For a breeze of morning moves,
And the planet of love is on high.

Alfred Tennyson

Today my resistance is:

Today my aspirations are:

Today's note to my baby:

Sunday

Though earth and moon

were gone

And suns and universes

ceased to be

And thou wert left alone

Every existence would exist

in thee

Emily Brontë

Flutterings! I am told that's what you will feel like. If I am still, I may perceive you. I shall lie here as motionless as I can. My thoughts flood by, and I neither hold them nor chase them. I neither grasp for you nor push you away. I am open in my stillness.

Today my limitations are:

Today my desire is:

Today's note to my baby:

Monday

I like being still with you. It is very serene. You are a good little teacher. Such delights are available when I am quiet. My inner life is not so vague. It becomes more real and ever so much more special than my daily, outward activities.

They are not flat surfaces
Having curved outlines,
They are round
Tapering toward the top.

Wallace Stevens

Today my denial is:

Today I am grateful for:

Today's note to my baby:

Tuesday

Where, like a pillow
on a bed,
A pregnant bank swelled
up, to rest
The violet's reclining head,
Sat we two one another's
best.

John Donne

I move about too much. Many of my doings are routine, habitual, purposeless. I bet you are not like that. You stretch and explore and then rest. Sometimes I just go and go and go till I think I'll collapse.

Today my heightened awareness is:

Today's reawakening is:

Today's note to my baby:

Wednesday

Today I'll watch the light. I'll pay attention to it all day, wherever I am, when it moves gradually and subtly and when it doesn't. When light grandly moves to dark or when a cloud unveils the sun abruptly, my mood alters drastically. I wonder how my brash movements affect you?

Listen, the wind is still,
And far away in the night
See the uplands fill
With a running light.

Mark Van Doren

Today my concern is:

Today I acknowledge:

Today's note to my baby:

Thursday

I'll do things evenly and with grace. I'll try to move like gradients of light bending throughout the day. Such a peaceful way to be: quiet and illuminated.

The pattern of the
atmosphere is spherical
A bubble is the silence
of the sun,
Blown thinner by the very
breath of miracle
Around a core of loud
confusion

Elinor Wylie

Today I want to avoid:

Today I want to address:

Today's note to my baby:

Friday

I wonder if the grand sun herself can penetrate my belly. Does she light your way? Do you glisten in delight and ride the bright amniotic waves?

When Earth repays with
golden sheaves
the labours of the plough,
And ripening fruits and
forest leaves
All brighten on the bough.

William Wordsworth

Today's vulnerability is:

Today my purpose is:

Today's note to my baby:

Saturday

The moon rains out her

beams, and heaven is

overflowed

Percy Bysshe Shelley

At night, the mesmerizing La Luna shines through all the blackness. Sometimes she is round and large and full—much like my belly. Her light softly sighs through the night. If I introduce you to her spell, you'll be chirruping in delight, and all the nights of your life she will call to you.

Today my need is:

Today my intuition is:

Today's note to my baby:

Sunday

Last month, you tripled in size; this month, you will only double. I hope that I don't mimic you. It is difficult getting used to my new body. I love the soft curves that you give me, yet sometimes I feel a bit anxious when I think in terms of distortion rather than a swell of life.

Today my resistance is:

Today my aspirations are:

Today's note to my baby:

Shall I find comfort,
travel-sore and weak?
Of labour you shall find
the sum.
Will there be beds for me
and all who seek?
Yea, beds for all who come.

Christina Georgina Rossetti

Monday

Beauty never slumbers;
All is in her name;
But the rose remembers
The dust from which it
  came.

  Edna St. Vincent Millay

Is it in this quiet month of being that your soul begins to form? As you stretch and move your arms and legs outward and position and reposition yourself, is there a place inside of you that remains apart, a place that reaches for the absolute, a place where you are extended into infinity?

Today my limitations are:

Today my desire is:

Today's note to my baby:

Tuesday

There is a place inside of me where my heart aligns with yours. A place that has nothing to do with our genes or my egg or your bloodline. It is an ancient place, where we meet in the darkness of all there is—a place where I unite with you in utter silence.

Something austere hides,
something uncertain
Beneath the deep bank
calls and makes quiet
music.

Dylan Thomas

Today my denial is:

....

Today I am grateful for:

....

Today's note to my baby:

Wednesday

We take this time to know each other and to be in the silence of each other. There will be many moments of speaking and touching and listening. Today, in the deep, restful quiet of my body and in the imponderable formation of your soul, I rest here at peace with you.

Radiant Sister of the day
Awake! Arise! and come
away!
To the wild woods and the
plains.

Percy Bysshe Shelley

Today my heightened awareness is:

Today's reawakening is:

Today's note to my baby:

Thursday

There is still a sacred hush about you. Your movements, like a distant rustle in a far-off bush, still elude me. I am content knowing that you are a joyous moment of all there is.

I have recovered it.

What? Eternity

It is the sea

Matched with the sun.

Francis Golffing

Today my concern is:

Today I acknowledge:

Today's note to my baby:

Friday

Let me believe in the clean

faith of the body,

The sweet glowing vigour,

And the gestures of

unageing love.

Dylan Thomas

Today I continue to honor you, and I try to slow my world to keep time with yours. It is a more peaceful way to be and a reminder that all things are possible.

Today I want to avoid:

Today I want to address:

Today's note to my baby:

Saturday

I enjoy the bond we share. You have helped to turn my focus from the outer world to a place much deeper and richer, a place I had forgotten for a while. Your being is imprinted on my soul.

There is sweet music here
that softer falls
than petals from blown
roses on the grass

Alfred Tennyson

Today's vulnerability is:

Today my purpose is:

Today's note to my baby:

Sunday

And sleep as I in childhood
* sweetly slept,*
Full of high thoughts,
* unborn, So let me lie—*
The grass below; above the
* vaulted sky.*

John Clare

Well, little embryonic rising, anatomy and physiology is your thing right now, and you are so gracious in sharing it with me. I can no longer sprawl on my back in wild abandon. It is not good for our circulation. Left side, pillow between my knees is our sleep position. I'm feeling a bit restricted.

Today my need is:

Today my intuition is:

Today's note to my baby:

Monday

I need a certain amount of expansion now other than in my belly. I've discovered regular daily exercise. One-half hour a day of stretching, walking, and rhythmic movements. This is great for both of us—you get more oxygen and nutrients transported, and I decrease fluid retention and facilitate your easy passage.

Today my resistance is:

Today my aspirations are:

Today's note to my baby:

Let me escape,
Be free (wind for my
  tree and water for
  my flower),
Live self for self,
And drown the gods
  in me,
or crush their viper
  heads beneath my foot
No space, no space,
  you say,
But you'll not keep me in,
Although your cage
  is strong

Dylan Thomas

Tuesday

All the seasons run

their race

In this quiet resting

place

Peach and apricot and

fig

Here will ripen and

grow big

Austin Dobson

Well, little cherub, I understand we are dealing with layers and coverings this month. My nails and my hair as well are growing rapidly. I even have a visible line down my abdomen; linea nigra is its official name. Your presence is influencing every aspect of my being.

Today my limitations are:

Today my desire is:

Today's note to my baby:

Wednesday

Your skin, delicate and translucent, is becoming thicker, hiding your blood vessels from view. I imagine your veins and their colorful rich lines like sea kelp—exquisite and visible. I hope your skin is thick, full, soft, and pliable, wonderfully protective and ever so gently receptive.

Today my denial is:

Today I am grateful for:

Today's note to my baby:

*I see from a distance
high and low
Winglike tiled roofs in
sunset's glow.
The coloured clouds
spread like brocade,
The river calm as silver
braid.*

Xie Tiao

Thursday

New cells are forming in the peripheral layers of your skin. You are being well prepared and packaged for the elements here. Such exciting things are in store for you. One morning, we'll collect the dew from the clover; close to the earth we'll bend. Later on, we'll run by the sea, and you'll feel the sand between your toes and the salty breeze on your flesh; your skin, wet from the water, will greet the sun.

Where the tread of many
    feet
Went trampling to and fro,
A child was born—speak
    low!
When the night and
    morning meet.

           Dora Greenwell

Today my heightened awareness is:

Today's reawakening is:

Today's note to my baby:

Friday

You waste nothing. Your dead skin cells are continually sloughing off and mixing with the oil from your skin glands—a great recipe, which becomes your vernix caseosa: an oily, cheese-like substance that gently coats your skin. Even you need protection from your environment. How self-sufficient to manufacture your own little wet suit. Surf well in your watery world.

Feast friends at left and
* right*
On cresses cooked so tender;
O bells and drums, delight
The babe so fair and slender!

Anonymous, Zhou Dynasty
(1112–256 B.C.E.)

Today my concern is:

Today I acknowledge:

Today's note to my baby:

Saturday

I feel the warmth of air

exhaled by coming

spring

As through my window

screen I hear the insects

sing.

Liu Fang-Ping

Your movements are becoming more forceful. Could your new coating be giving you improved confidence and a greater ability to slosh about? Have fun! I shall pay careful attention to your movements. This is your first communication to me. I am aware and present and feeling you.

Today I want to avoid:

Today I want to address:

Today's note to my baby:

Sunday

The skin on your palms and the soles of your feet is becoming thicker. With your bare hands and bare feet you can touch and explore and feel the world.

The fields grew fatter day
by day,
The wild fowl of the air
increased

William Butler Yeats

Today's vulnerability is:

Today my purpose is:

Today's note to my baby:

Monday

How can you leave upon

my mind no trace?

Secluded heart creates

secluded place.

Tao Qian

Well, we can now practice a bit of palmistry. Your life line is developing, reflecting the formation of your digestive and respiratory system. May your line be deep, clean, long, and unbroken: à votre santé.

Today my need is:

Today my intuition is:

Today's note to my baby:

Tuesday

The middle line on your palm reflects the development of your nervous system. I wish you a strong and balanced constitution and a deep, intuitive awareness of yourself and others.

Today my resistance is:

Today my aspirations are:

Today's note to my baby:

No need of motion or
of strength,
Or even the breathing air:
I thought of Nature's
loveliest scenes;
And with memory
I was there.

Dorothy Wordsworth

Wednesday

In my most secret spirit
grew
A whirling and a wandering
fire:
I stood: keen stars above
me shone.

William Butler Yeats

Another palm line—the uppermost—is also developing, which reflects the development of your circulatory and excretory systems. May you let wisdom and joy flow through you, and may you excrete all that is evil and negative.

Today my limitations are:

Today my desire is:

Today's note to my baby:

Thursday

May all three lines on your palm representing the major systems of your body coordinate smoothly, integrate easily, and genuinely reflect a well-developed clarity and strength of being.

The sky remains infinitely vacant for earth there to build its heaven with dreams.

Rabindranath Tagore

Today my denial is:

Today I am grateful for:

Today's note to my baby:

Friday

When night comes on in,
unto our home we go,
Our corn we carry, and
our infant too
Weary indeed!
So many things for our
attendance call
Had we ten hands we could
employ them all.

Mary Collier

In case you weren't aware of it, my growing fetus, according to Chinese medicine, your right palm reflects all my heritage. Your maternal grand-mother, my mother, influences your digestive and respiratory line. I haven't the vaguest idea what kind of eating binges she indulged in. Let's hope she liked grains and nuts and that she craved an occasional carrot for good luck.

Today my heightened awareness is:

Today's reawakening is:

Today's note to my baby:

Saturday

Well, I'm still focusing on your right palm; quite an intricate development. Your maternal grandfather has an influence on your nervous system line. May your nervous system thrive on peace and serenity.

I am the one whose praise
echoes on high.
I adorn all the earth

Hildegard von Bingen

Today my concern is:

Today I acknowledge:

Today's note to my baby:

Sunday

Billows murmurs
*   at our feet*
Where earth and
*   ocean meet,*
And all things seem
*   only one*
In the universal sun.

Percy Bysshe Shelley

Now let's consider your left palm. Well at least I'm not responsible for the lines on this one—this side reflects your father's heritage. May all your lines be deep and clear.

Today I want to avoid:

Today I want to address:

Today's note to my baby:

Monday

Your little hands are amazing; they tell so very much about you. May they reflect the constitutional strength I so desire for you. I can't wait to kiss each finger, each line. My wish for your palms is that they know love and healing and discretion.

Today's vulnerability is:

Today my purpose is:

Today's note to my baby:

Child, thou bringest
to my heart
the babble of the wind
and water,
the flower's speechless
secrets, the cloud's
dreams,
the mute gaze of wonder
of the morning sky

Rabindranath Tagore

Tuesday

Dear little saint of my life,

Deep in my breasts I feel

The warm milk come to

   birth.

   Federico Garcia Lorca

You have been taking in proteins, fats, and minerals, and you are now discharging them in the form of fine hair. You are in balance. What an amazing little system you have.

Today my need is:

Today my intuition is:

Today's note to my baby:

Wednesday

Spirals of hair are developing on your skull; the main one is at the crown of your head. Do draw in the heavenly forces. May your body be filled with a divine energy, your own true self.

I am gone into the fields
To take what this sweet
hour yields.

Percy Bysshe Shelley

Today my resistance is:

Today my aspirations are:

Today's note to my baby:

Thursday

He that question would
   anew
What fair Eden was of old,
Let him rightly study you,
And a brief of that behold.
Welcome, welcome,
   then . . .

Robert Herrick

Now you also have soft, fine hair on your back and arms and legs. A gently furry creature you are.

Today my limitations are:

Today my desire is:

Today's note to my baby:

Friday

Your soft covering of hair has a name. It is known as lanugo. So fine and downy it is. You'll probably shed it all in your first week of life.

A mind at peace
with all below,
A heart whose love is
innocent!

Lord Byron

Today my denial is:

Today I am grateful for:

Today's note to my baby:

Saturday

Sleep my babe; thy food

and raiment,

House and home, thy

friends provide;

All without thy care

or payment:

All thy wants are well

supplied.

Isaac Watts

Now you're also swallowing bits of your hair and a little of your vernix caseosa, all contained in your amniotic fluid. Some of this you can absorb through your digestive tract. It doesn't sound too palatable—but then again, neither does animal meat, which I've eaten or at least had offered to me.

Today my heightened awareness is:

Today's reawakening is:

Today's note to my baby:

Sunday

This is our halfway point. If you go to full term, you will be born forty weeks from day one of my last menstrual period. May your body, well dressed in an amniotic veil, continue to thrive.

The whole world is here
  on my body
Multiple coloralities
    bursting into spirit
Which is me.

Ruth Lerner

Today my concern is:

Today I acknowledge:

Today's note to my baby:

Monday

No puddings just shouldings

No chocolate and goodings

Just raisins and kumquats

And spinach and green

*   squash.*

Eugenia Persico

I must continue to ensure that you get all the ingredients you need.

A Perfectly Balanced Meal:

½   cup almonds or ¼ cup sesame tahini or almond butter

8   ounces cottage cheese, milk, or yogurt

½   cup brown rice or ½ bagel

¾   cup spinach, asparagus, kale, or mustard greens

¾   cup yellow squash or carrots

4   ounces cantaloupe or watermelon

Today I want to avoid:

Today I want to address:

Today's note to my baby:

Tuesday

It's difficult to drink eight glasses (eight ounces each) of water daily. It is necessary in order to support the increase in my blood volume and to maintain your amniotic fluid, so I shall try to maintain this fluid intake. Freshly squeezed juice and milk are okay too, but no soda, tea, coffee, or alcohol. A cup of hot water is actually quite soothing.

Today's vulnerability is:

Today my purpose is:

Today's note to my baby:

You send forth springs into the gullies,
They wind their way between the mountains,
Giving drink to all the animals,
The trees of the lord drink their fill
The stork makes her home among the junipers.

Psalm 104

Wednesday

This halfway mark is reminding me of all I have to do. Sometimes I forget to exercise the muscle between my pubic bone in front to my tail bone (coccyx) in the back. Its colloquial name is the Kegel muscle.

I sought to greet the dawn

with music

And to worship the

morning with song

In my hands I held the lyre

and the pipe

And my left hand moved

skillfully over the strings

I tied the timbrel and the

flute to my side and

adjusted their loops.

Now tightening,

now loosening them

Meshullam Da Piera

Today my need is:

Today my intuition is:

Today's note to my baby:

Thursday

If my Kegel is weak, it can't support your uterine home. If it's strong, it helps my bowel and bladder control. To exercise this muscle, I tighten it as if to prevent urination. I must do this in sets of five at least ten times a day.

Today my resistance is:

Today my aspirations are:

Today's note to my baby:

Your curved thighs are like Jewels fashioned by a master. Your navel is a round goblet brim full of wine. Your belly is a heap of wheat Ringed with lilies.

Seventh century B.C.E.
Hebrew text

Friday

How beautiful the Buddhist

Statues

At Sagu

Half hidden in falling

leaves

Imaizumi Sogetsu-Ni

Rest well beneath my heart chamber. My heart beats so much more slowly than yours.

Today my limitations are:

Today my desire is:

Today's note to my baby:

Saturday

I continue to exercise daily, yet not so strenuously as before. It feels right to decrease my pace.

Today my denial is:

Today I am grateful for:

Today's note to my baby:

The leaves of the lush
*   clover rustle in the wind.*
I, not a leaf
Watched you without
*   a sound.*
You may have thought I
*   paid no attention.*

Kenrei Mon-in Ukyo
no Daibu

Sunday

Like all vessels, fragile

Like all vessels too small

for the destiny poured

into it.

Rosario Castellanos

Some of your intake is indigestible, and your large intestine accumulates your waste in the form of a watery feces known as meconium (it sounds like a rare ore).

Today my heightened awareness is:

Today's reawakening is:

Today's note to my baby:

Monday

Such delicate waste, your meconium. The secretion of your bile into your intestinal tract causes it to take on a dark green color. I understand that all of this usually stays in your intestine until shortly after birth, when you discharge your uterine feedings. Will I get to change your first diaper?

Today my concern is:

Today I acknowledge:

Today's note to my baby:

As a sweet organ
* harmony strikes*
*   the ear*
So, for the primal mind,
* my eyes receive*
A vision of your future
* drawing near.*

Dante Alighieri

Tuesday

Now you weigh practically two pounds. I'm a little ahead of you in gaining weight. However, I'm focusing on my nutrition and not on weight gain. Cheers to a bit of maternal fat.

Our toil and labour's
daily so extreme
That we have hardly
any time to dream.

Mary Collier

Today I want to avoid:

Today I want to address:

Today's note to my baby:

Wednesday

My, you are growing! The average length of your peers is thirteen inches long. That means you're a tad more than a ruler. Do you ever just feel like stretching as far as you can?

Today's vulnerability is:

Today my purpose is:

Today's note to my baby:

Moon of the Ninth
* Month*
Cast its shadow.
How weary is the life
* within*
When it sees its dark
* prison*
It struggles to be free
And make its camp
* on earth*

Native American
birthing song

Thursday

Your skin is thin right now. You are so very fragile. I'm glad that you are well cushioned. I close my eyes and breathe a gentle caress across your flesh.

Day by day thy shadow

shines in heaven beholden;

Even the sun, the shining

shadow of thy face.

Algernon Charles Swinburne

Today my need is:

Today my intuition is:

Today's note to my baby:

Friday

I understand that your covering is shiny. That makes me think that it is pulled taut across your being. I wonder what you feel and whether you are comfortable in your commencement suit.

So I shall make little fool homes with doors, always open Doors for all and each to run away where they want to.

Carl Sandburg

Today my resistance is:

Today my aspirations are:

Today's note to my baby:

Saturday

Come for the soul is free!

In all the vast dreamland

There is no lock for thee,

Each door awaits thy hand.

Bliss Corman

Now your fingers and toes are printed as yours. Such definition you are developing! I hope you place your fingerprints with care and grace as you journey through these lands.

Today my limitations are:

Today my desire is:

Today's note to my baby:

Sunday

Your eyelids are beginning to part. Take a peak at your surroundings, and let your eyes be flooded by the rich fluid of your drift.

Vernal fruitions and desires
are linked in endless
chase;
While as one kindly
growth retires,
Another takes its place.

William Wordsworth

Today my denial is:

Today I am grateful for:

Today's note to my baby:

Monday

Hug me round

In your solitude

Profound

Georgia Douglas Johnson

Well, I understand that you have barely any fat under your glistening skin. You do, however, have much protection and other kinds of coats and layers.

Today my heightened awareness is:

Today's reawakening is:

Today's note to my baby:

Tuesday

I don't know why, but when I think of you without any underlying fat, I want to protect you even more. I think I'll buy you a beautiful shawl today: warm, soft, beautifully textured, and white.

Here are threads, my true
love, fine as silk,
To knit thee, to knit thee,
A pair of stockings white
as milk.

Anonymous

Today my concern is:

Today I acknowledge:

Today's note to my baby:

Wednesday

We couldn't be closer than we are now, and yet I long for the ability to protect you and caress you and cradle you in my arms. You feel a bit far away, as the constancy of my own heart does.

A heart as soft,
a heart as kind,
A heart as sound and free
As in the whole world thou
canst find,
That heart I'll give to thee.

Robert Herrick

Today I want to avoid:

Today I want to address:

Today's note to my baby:

Thursday

Another way I can protect you is to keep your amnion strong by eating well. How about something dark, green, and leafy for lunch today? Cooked spinach, chard, escarole, or bok choy, and a sprout salad, with a mound of tofu or cottage cheese for protein.

There from the tree
We'll cherries pluck, and
pick the strawberry.

Thomas Randolph

....

Today's vulnerability is:

....

Today my purpose is:

....

Today's note to my baby:

Friday

So I understand that you are sipping amniotic fluid on a daily basis. It's rather salty, as I recall (it was once my liquid diet, too). Let's drink to your health. I'll have carrot and beet juice with a tad of ginger. I'm a bit tired, and it's a great energizer.

What is this life,

if full of care,

We have no time to stand

and stare?

William Henry Davies

Today my need is:

Today my intuition is:

Today's note to my baby:

Saturday

You have fluttering eyelashes now, all wet and beautiful, and eyebrows to go with them. You're becoming more and more complete day by day. There's certainly nothing routine about your days.

Everyone suddenly burst
out singing;
And I was filled with such
delight.

Siegfried Sassoon

Today my resistance is:

Today my aspirations are:

Today's note to my baby:

Sunday

Let the dark walls that

enclose you

tumble down!

Receive the lap of your

mother the earth.

Rosario Castellanos

Your lips are distinct this month. I'd love to see you grin from ear to ear. May your mouth be generous, loving, warm, and expressive.

Today my limitations are:

Today my desire is:

Today's note to my baby:

Monday

You are well proportioned at this stage of your life. I do hope that continues into your old age. I feel a bit out of proportion right now, so I'm glad one of us is in balance.

She walks up the walk
Like a woman in a dream,
She forgets she borrowed
* butter*
And pays you back cream!

Edna St. Vincent Millay

Today my denial is:

Today I am grateful for:

Today's note to my baby:

Tuesday

Your eyes are developed, but your iris still lacks pigment. At birth, your eyes will be similar to those of the other "neonates" (that's what you'll be called, you know); their color will not be as sharp or clear as they will be when you are a bit older.

But if ye sow that which no

eyes can see,

The inward beauty of her

lively sprite,

Garnisht with heavenly

guifts of high degree,

Much more then would ye

wonder at the sight,

And stand astonisht.

Edmund Spenser

Today my heightened awareness is:

Today's reawakening is:

Today's note to my baby:

Wednesday

With your eyes barely open, you experience the nature surrounding you. One day, we shall look at the stars together and laugh with the new moon.

Therefore awake! Make
*   haste, I say*
And let us; without staying.
All in our gowns of green
*   so gay*
Into the park a-maying.

                    Anonymous

Today my concern is:

Today I acknowledge:

Today's note to my baby:

Thursday

You are growing and are enclosed in my womb, yet you know no limitations. May your experience always be one of timeless and boundless energy.

That then, is loveliness,
we said,
Children in wonder watching
the stars,
Is the aim at the end.

Dylan Thomas

....

Today I want to avoid:

....

Today I want to address:

....

Today's note to my baby:

Friday

I send you my unbounded love and energy. I am here for you. You are so calm inside me. You bring me a deep sense of inner peace, and I send it back to you. Such lovely reciprocity.

Love is the perfect sum
Of all delight

Anonymous

Today's vulnerability is:

Today my purpose is:

Today's note to my baby:

Saturday

Earlier this week, I felt out of proportion and a bit out of balance. When I meditate on the perfection of you, my enthusiasm soars and I feel at one with your limitless potential.

Thy walls are made of

precious stones,

Thy bulwarks diamonds

square;

Thy gates are of bright

orient pearl;

Exceedingly rich and rare.

Anonymous

Today my need is:

Today my intuition is:

Today's note to my baby:

Sunday

Sometimes I feel as though I need more support than I am receiving right now. I know this feeling is normal, but knowing that doesn't always help me feel better.

Today my resistance is:

Today my aspirations are:

Today's note to my baby:

A measure of holiness
a measure of power
A measure of fearfulness
a measure of terror
A measure of trembling
a measure of shaking
A measure of awe

Third century A.D.
Hebrew text

Monday

Sometimes I feel very alone. No one can participate as I really want them to, because only I am carrying you.

Then I considered all of this and through me And through no other all came into being So the end will come through me and through no other.

100 A.D. Latin text

Today my limitations are:

Today my desire is:

Today's note to my baby:

Tuesday

I wish your father would reassure me that he feels as deep a bond with you as I do.

So come to me now, free me
   from this aching pain,
Fulfill everything that
My heart desires to be
   fulfilled; you, yes you,
   will be my ally.

Sappho

Today my denial is:

Today I am grateful for:

Today's note to my baby:

Wednesday

To look at you gives joy;

your eyes are like honey,

Love flows over your gentle

face . . .

Sappho

I need more physical involvement with your daddy. Some of my desires may be overwhelming to him right now.

Today my heightened awareness is:

Today's reawakening is:

Today's note to my baby:

Thursday

Can I ever feel totally independent? I move from needing my mother to needing my husband.

The stars pass
The moon passes
Blue clouds pass above the
   mountains to the north
The years go by

Empress Jito

Today my concern is:

Today I acknowledge:

Today's note to my baby:

Friday

On the road through

the clouds

Is there a short cut

To the summer moon?

Den Sute-Jo

Now is not the time for distance. It is a time for forgiveness and closeness.

Today I want to avoid:

Today I want to address:

Today's note to my baby:

Saturday

I desire connection: physical, spiritual, and emotional. Social support is especially important to me now.

Let love embrace the ten thousand things;
Heaven and earth are a simple body.

Hai Shih

Today's vulnerability is:

Today my purpose is:

Today's note to my baby:

Sunday

Mingling me and thee;

When like light of eyes

Flashed through thee

   and me

Truth shall make us free

Liberty make wise.

Algernon Charles Swinburne

It is with great clarity that I hear the ring of your being inside of me.

Today my need is:

Today my intuition is:

Today's note to my baby:

Monday

The path between you and me is alive. You are the expansive bridge between mind and spirit.

Goddess and maiden and queen, be near me now and befriend.

Algernon Charles Swinburne

Today my resistance is:

Today my aspirations are:

Today's note to my baby:

Tuesday

When thy beauty

appears

In its graces and airs

All bright as an angel

new dropped from

the sky,

At distance I gaze and

am awed by my

fears,

So strangely you dazzle

my eye.

Thomas Parnell

As you gestate within my womb, you make me know that all things are possible.

....

Today my limitations are: ·

....

Today my desire is:

....

Today's note to my baby:

Wednesday

Your world is shifting now to one of sound. You can hear all the rumblings going on in your womb palace. I try to stay calm and centered in hopes that my heart beats rhythmically and makes you feel safe.

Today my denial is:

Today I am grateful for:

Today's note to my baby:

*Hush! my dear, lie still
    and slumber
Holy angels guard
    thy bed!
Heavenly blessings
    without number
gently falling on
    thy head.*

Isaac Watts

Thursday

You can hear voices now. I shall read aloud to you. I understand you like repetition. I'll pick out a few books today and begin to read to you daily. Then, when you're born and I read to you, you'll remember and you'll be comforted.

Today my heightened awareness is:

Today's reawakening is:

Today's note to my baby:

Friday

According to most studies, you and your unborn friends have a prefer-
ence for Vivaldi: your fetal heart becomes steady, and your kicking
declines when you listen to his music.

Here in valleys cool
and green,
Far ahead the thrush
is seen.

Austin Dobson

Today my concern is:

Today I acknowledge:

Today's note to my baby:

Saturday

Heart to heart as we lay
In the dawning of the day.

Robert Bridges

You seem to like the largo movements of most baroque music. We can enjoy lovely relaxation together. Surrounded by such beauty, we listen undisturbed; our hearts beat restfully. I shall sing our song to you today.

Today I want to avoid:

Today I want to address:

Today's note to my baby:

Sunday

Now your brain is becoming mature enough that my behavior can be experienced by you emotionally. This is a new responsibility. Now I must deal with any ambivalence that I have about being a mother so I can send you all the warmth and love you deserve.

Today's vulnerability is:

Today my purpose is:

Today's note to my baby:

O world invisible,
  we view thee,
O world intangible,
  we touch thee,
O world unknowable,
  we know thee,
Inapprehensible,
  we clutch thee!

Francis Thompson

Monday

Airly beacon, airly beacon,

O the happy hours we lay

Deep in fern on airly

beacon

Courting through the

summer's day.

Arthur Hugh Clough

Your daddy has a big responsibility now also. If his voice is any less than loving to me, then not only are you annoyed by the sound of it but you also experience the result of my feelings. We need to be surrounded with peaceful, loving, and supportive people.

Today my need is:

Today my intuition is:

Today's note to my baby:

Tuesday

I'll make certain you know that I love you. I'll continue to stroke my abdomen often. You like that. I'll eat very healthy foods. Of course, I'll continue not to drink alcohol, coffee, and soft drinks. I wouldn't dream of smoking a cigarette or marijuana or of taking any other drugs, even over the counter—not even a simple aspirin will I take. I'll try my best not to harm you in any way.

Sweet babe, in thy face
Soft desires I can trace,
Secret joys and secret
*   smiles,*
Little pretty infant wiles.

William Blake

Today my resistance is:

Today my aspirations are:

Today's note to my baby:

Wednesday

I know that you send me messages by the way you kick and move about. I know most music upsets you except baroque. I know Daddy's voice agitates you when it's loud. Even a bright light shining on my abdomen stresses you. At this stage, if I sunbathe I'll cover you gently. I can show you love by listening to your gentle communications and heeding them.

Beauty sat bathing by
*   a spring,*
Where forest shades did
*   hide her,*
The winds blew calm, the
*   birds did sing*
The cool streams ran
*   beside her.*

Anthony Munday

Today my limitations are:

Today my desire is:

Today's note to my baby:

Thursday

Sometimes my emotions are so muted that I'm not quite aware of them. Another way I can be there for you and for me is to listen to my dreams and to work on understanding them. You may have subtle and sympathetic communications. You and I share such an amazing bond. I wonder what you feel when I sing our song to you.

The birds around me
hopped and played
Their thoughts I cannot
measure:
But the least motion
which they made,
It seemed a thrill of
pleasure.

William Wordsworth

Today my denial is:

Today I am grateful for:

Today's note to my baby:

Friday

Here are reeds, my true

love, fine and neat,

To make thee,

to make thee,

A bonnet to withstand

the heat.

Anonymous

You know that I can't be perfect. There are going to be times when I am upset and when certain events cause me to feel stressed. However, I make this commitment to you: I shall not ignore you physically or psychologically on a consistent basis. I'll do the best that I can to give you a healthy environment. Peaceful floatings.

Today my heightened awareness is:

Today's reawakening is:

Today's note to my baby:

Saturday

Well, here we are, sending messages back and forth to each other. We are in this together. I guess the more I understand my own feelings, the more I can understand and respect yours. Silence is important. Let's try that now. I'll be quiet and will sit absolutely still for five minutes. I'll focus on my breath.

We dance round in a ring
and suppose,
But the secret sits in the
middle and knows.

Robert Frost

Today my concern is:

Today I acknowledge:

Today's note to my baby:

Sunday

The tender infant who
was long
A prisoner of fond fears;
But now, when every
sharp-edged blast
Is quiet in its sheath,
His mother leaves him free
to taste
Earth's sweetness in thy
breath.

William Wordsworth

Being quiet together yesterday was lovely. I think we should do that daily. Silent and serene, in a deep bond of love.

Today I want to avoid:

Today I want to address:

Today's note to my baby:

This channel filled with reassurance that we have flowing between us is another part of protecting you from all the uncertainties that you will encounter. The work we do in our silent time together is more important than all the politicians realize. They could learn from us.

How small a part of time
they share
That are so wondrous
sweet and fair!

Edmund Waller

Today's vulnerability is:

Today my purpose is:

Today's note to my baby:

Tuesday

So far from sweet real things
my thoughts had strayed,
I had forgot wide fields and
clear broad streams,
The perfect loveliness that
God has made,
Wild violets shy and heaven-
mounting dreams
And now unwittingly,
you've made me dream

Alice Dunbar Moore Nelson

In you and I lie the origins of society. Our relationship affects all our attitudes toward life. Your arms, legs, eyes, ears, and blood vessels are distinctly individual. You are unique, as is our relationship.

Today my need is:

Today my intuition is:

Today's note to my baby:

Wednesday

We are repeating evolution. Since your conception, your nervous system and your brain have become increasingly complex.

"Lo I am dark, but

comely," Sheba sings.

"And we were black," three

sheiks reply, "but kings."

Countee Cullen

Today my resistance is:

Today my aspirations are:

Today's note to my baby:

Thursday

I will gather pens, my lovely
one,
To put in thy lap.

Anonymous

Your brain is impressive. Daily your cortex increases, and you get new grooves and ridges. What a cellular delight!

Today my limitations are:

Today my desire is:

Today's note to my baby:

Friday

My brain in some sense regulates yours, and your brain regulates the functioning of your organs. I offer you social awareness and centered emotional responses, as you have offered me a connection to the universal cosmic consciousness.

Today my denial is:

Today I am grateful for:

Today's note to my baby:

*Symbolic mother, we thy
    myriad sons,
Pounding our stubborn
    hearts on Freedom bars,
Clutching our birthright,
    fight with faces set,
Still visioning the stars.*

Jessie Redmond Fouset

Saturday

The high, the low, the rich,
   the poor,
The black, the white,
   the red,
And all the chromatique
   between,
Of whom shall it be said:
Here lies the dust of Africa.

Georgia Douglas Johnson

I love that you reverberate just like an endless hymn.

Today my heightened awareness is:

Today's reawakening is:

Today's note to my baby:

Sunday

You reach and grasp with every bit of your being. I imagine and focus and push into what I think is infinite capacity, where at last I have grasped the endless—and then there you go again, taking boundless leaps.

Deep, deep our love, too
deep to show
Deep, deep we drink; silent
we grow.

Du Mu

Today my concern is:

Today I acknowledge:

Today's note to my baby:

Monday

We were very tired, we were very merry
We had gone back and forth all night on the ferry.

Edna St. Vincent Millay

We play together in the night. You kick and crawl in wondrous ceremony. Then you turn inside me. You magnetically draw me forward. Then you leap and bound once more.

Today I want to avoid:

Today I want to address:

Today's note to my baby:

Tuesday

I know that I shall silently meet you again today or tonight and that I shall feel you circulate and frolic in the splendor of your heights. I shall feel you dance and swim and leap inside my womb.

Today's vulnerability is:

Today my purpose is:

Today's note to my baby:

I have lived with you some
hours of the night,
The late hour,
When the lights lower,
The later hour,
When the lights go out.

John Peale Bishop

Wednesday

You are an endless stretch of wondrous breath. A rising hush of all there is. I delight in you.

Surely, I said,

Now will the poets sing.

But they have raised no cry

I wonder why.

Countee Cullen

....

Today my need is:

....

Today my intuition is:

....

Today's note to my baby:

Thursday

You float and rise in me. You whisper fathomless invitations, and I hear the echo of your form, sweet and ancient in the night.

Let me go forth, and share
The overflowing sun.

Robert Bridges

Today my resistance is:

Today my aspirations are:

Today's note to my baby:

Friday

I caress my belly; we are as one. Then you playfully flip and kick once more, making way for your independence. I look directly at you, and you kiss me softly with your knee.

Slips and pulls the

table cloth

Overturns a coffee-cup,

Reorganised upon the floor

She yawns and draws a

stocking up.

T. S. Eliot

Today my limitations are:

Today my desire is:

Today's note to my baby:

Saturday

I realize that our biological connection is critical and that the quality of the nutrients I ingest determine your physical and mental constitution. I delight in all the possibilities of our intuitive communication.

Time, milk, and magic from the world beginning.

Dylan Thomas

Today my denial is:

Today I am grateful for:

Today's note to my baby:

Sunday

While the imagination
    strains after deer
Going by fields of
    goldenrod in
The stifling heat of
September.

William Carlos Williams

Your blood, cells, tissues, organs, and amniotic fluid are renewed by my food intake. Today we'll dine on brown rice, carrots, butternut squash, collard greens, lentils, and tofu. We'll toast with miso soup. Here's to your balanced constitution. Oh, for a glass of wine, some provolone, a large piece of rich dark chocolate; then a long swim in a tropical sea, comfortable and thin in my new bikini.

Today my heightened awareness is:

Today's reawakening is:

Today's note to my baby:

Monday

Well, our good nutrition has paid off. You are beginning to have some fat deposited under your skin. That makes you just a bit more cuddly.

Radishes and lettuce
Eggplants and beets
Turnips fo' de winter
an' candied sweets.

Sterling Allen Brown

Today my concern is:

Today I acknowledge:

Today's note to my baby:

Tuesday

A glass pitcher,
    the tumbler
Turned down, by which
A key is lying—and the
Immaculate white bed.

William Carlos Williams

I've seen pictures of unborns your age sucking their thumb. Soon you'll have other choices. My breasts are full and ready for you.

Today I want to avoid:

Today I want to address:

Today's note to my baby:

Wednesday

Sometimes I feel you hiccup. Just because the volume of your amniotic fluid is diminishing doesn't mean you have to gulp it. Relax, little wonder. Soon you'll taste the sweet milk of my breast instead of the salty fluid of your amniotic ocean.

Today's vulnerability is:

Today my purpose is:

Today's note to my baby:

When strawberries go begging, and the sleek
Blue plums lie open to the blackbird's beak,
We shall live well—we shall live very well.

Elinor Wylie

Thursday

I look forward to feeding you, to holding you in my arms and letting you suck. I feel a bit tired of being pregnant, and sometimes I worry about you. It seems that it will be easier to care for you when I can see you. I guess seeing is just a more familiar way of being and knowing.

Give to these children new

   from the world,

Silence and love

And the long dew-dropping

   hours of the night,

And the stars above.

William Butler Yeats

Today my need is:

Today my intuition is:

Today's note to my baby:

Friday

I hope your placenta is growing properly so that it can give to you all the oxygen and nutrients that you need.

I sigh that I kiss you,
For I must own
That I shall miss you
When you have grown.

William Butler Yeats

....

Today my resistance is:

....

Today my aspirations are:

....

Today's note to my baby:

Saturday

And then I shall lift up to

thee my little hand

And thou shalt think thine

heart in ease.

Anonymous

About your umbilical arteries: are they able to get rid of all the waste products? May you always be able to let go of all that is unnecessary so that you can maintain your peace and happiness.

Today my limitations are:

Today my desire is:

Today's note to my baby:

Sunday

Now you weigh about three pounds and you are about seventeen inches long. You still have a lot of growing to do, with only ten weeks left till your debut.

My heart is high above;
my body is full of bliss,
For I am set in luve as well
as I would wiss.

Anonymous

Today my denial is:

Today I am grateful for:

Today's note to my baby:

Monday

Hourly I sigh,

For all things are leaf-like

And cloud-like

Dylan Thomas

I feel you kicking within me. Sometimes your movements are soft and gentle like the flutter of miniature angel's wings, and I smile and touch you. Can you feel me?

Today my heightened awareness is:

Today's reawakening is:

Today's note to my baby:

Tuesday

Sometimes you seem rather playful and frisky; at other moments you seem to be trying to find the best and most comfortable position. I hope your umbilical cord doesn't get in your way.

No time to stand beneath the boughs
And stare as long as sheep or cows.

William Henry Davies

Today my concern is:

Today I acknowledge:

Today's note to my baby:

Wednesday

All the seasons run their

race

In this quiet resting place

Peach and apricot and fig

Here will ripen and

grow big

Austin Dobson

I feel you again deep within me, and suddenly a wave of you ripples across the ever so open silence.

Today I want to avoid:

Today I want to address:

Today's note to my baby:

Thursday

Like a barefoot gypsy beckoning the flamenco dancer from the cobble-stone path to the soft-soled plains, you listen to the song I sing to you and roll and tumble quietly and rhythmically.

Far off, the still bamboo
Grows green; the desert
*   pool*
Turns gaudy turquoise for
*   the chanting caravan.*

Wallace Stevens

....
Today's vulnerability is:

....
Today my purpose is:

....
Today's note to my baby:

Friday

Take if you must, this little

bag of dreams;

Unloose the cord, and they

will wrap you round.

William Butler Yeats

The night high in the vastness of the sky
Soothes and rocks her midnight world.
As in a bassinet, wrapped in the soft cotton robes of a cloud,
You inhale the veil of saviour darkness and breathe out into my womb
bounding leaps of joy.

Today my need is:

Today my intuition is:

Today's note to my baby:

Saturday

I feel you, and I am at times overwhelmed and I feel unable and perhaps a bit unwilling to fathom you and me and our connection.

Today my resistance is:

Today my aspirations are:

Today's note to my baby:

Flow on, river! Flow with
the flood tide, and ebb
with the ebb tide!
Frolic on, crested and
scallop-edged waves!
Gorgeous clouds of the
sunset! drench with
your splendor, me.

Carl Sandburg

Sunday

Give to these children new

from the world,

Rest far from men!

William Butler Yeats

You are well cushioned by your amniotic fluid.
I send my voice rippling across your waters.
What name shall I call to you child of mine,
What name shall I sing to your ears,
And how shall you look sweet child of mine,
And can I allay all your fears?

Today my limitations are:

Today my desire is:

Today's note to my baby:

Monday

You must stay in my womb now. This is a crucial time, to prevent the possibility of your being born premature. It's safe in there, I hope. I listen carefully for your subtle communications.

Today my denial is:

Today I am grateful for:

Today's note to my baby:

And I am free to know
That you are bound to
   me only by choice,
   that you are bound
   to me by love,
And I am finally
Out of control.

Helen Whitaker

Tuesday

Amazing nuances of development are occurring. The muscles of your chest wall and diaphragm, enabling you to expand and contract during breathing, are being fine-tuned.

Arabesques of candle

beams,

Winding

Through our heavy

dreams

Wallace Stevens

Today my heightened awareness is:

Today's reawakening is:

Today's note to my baby:

Wednesday

The reflex centers of your brain, which coordinate your muscles for breathing and for swallowing, are beginning to function.

The red rose whispers
of passion,
And the white rose breathes
of love;
Oh, the red rose is a falcon
And the white rose is
a dove.

John Boyle O'Reilly

Today my concern is:

Today I acknowledge:

Today's note to my baby:

Thursday

Methinks ofttimes my
heart is like some bee
That goes forth through the
summer days and sings,
And gathers honey from all
growing things
In garden plot or in the
clover lea.

Ella Wheeler Wilcox

Again I realize how important my diet is in providing the optimum development of your nervous system and the many dimensions of your mind/body.

Today I want to avoid:

Today I want to address:

Today's note to my baby:

Friday

I try not to worry, as it is not healthy for either of us, but nutrition is so very important, especially iron and vitamin B12 to prevent anemia. I've developed a taste for pumpkin seeds, sesame seeds, and sunflower seeds. I've been told to eat whole grains of millet and buckwheat, sea vegetables, and soybeans. Cooked white fish is good for you and me too.

But deep in the center
of my heart,
A small ember glows
waiting for the breath
of life
to fan it into flames.

Helen Whitaker

Today's vulnerability is:

Today my purpose is:

Today's note to my baby:

Saturday

And it's green, green, green
all the happy night
and day;
Green of leaf and green of
sod, green of ivy on
the wall.
And the blessed Irish
shamrock with the
fairest green of all.

Mary Elizabeth McGrath
Blake

Calcium is also very important in our diet. Cheese is good, but it's a bit fattening. I'm getting used to nonfat cottage cheese. I realize that sea vegetables are good for everything; the Japan Nutritionist Association has known for years that hijiki, wakame, and arame are top drawer in most nutrients. I'm off to shop for them again today so we can maintain them as a staple in our food plan. I am not used to their taste yet, but I hear I can make a powder of them and use it as a sprinkle. Ah, such a life you lead. You just lie there and take it all in.

Today my need is:

Today my intuition is:

Today's note to my baby:

Sunday

I found out that you have a new trick. You can now turn your head from side to side. I just turned mine—I never realized before how amazing that must be when you do it for the first time.

Today my resistance is:

Today my aspirations are:

Today's note to my baby:

So lithe and delicate—
So slender is thy state,
So pale and pure thy face,
So deer-like in their grace
Thy limbs, that all do vie
To take and charm the eye.

James Herbert Morse

Monday

A fire-mist and a planet
A crystal and a cell,
A jelly fish and a saurian,
And caves where the
cave-men dwell;
Then a sense of law and
beauty,
And a face turned from
the clod;
Some call it evolution
And others call it God.

William Herbert Carruta

You're a bit more rounded this week, and I'm so happy you're still inside me. Please stay until you've reached term. It's a lot safer that way.

Today my limitations are:

Today my desire is:

Today's note to my baby:

Tuesday

Your skin is now covered with white grease—your own little intrauterine outfit. May your worldly sense of fashion be as natural and creative.

Today my denial is:

Today I am grateful for:

Today's note to my baby:

O you mad rag Czars!
If you would see us and
clothe us as we truly are
Look to the moon!
Call all her phases full and
Give us clothes
to celebrate her
Week by week, month by
month
Cycle by cycle.

Ruth Lerner

Wednesday

One sigh—and then the
lib'rant morn
Of perfect day,
When my free spirit, newly
born,
Will soar away!

William Winter

It's really important for me to massage my skin all over, especially my perineum and breasts. Sesame oil is so soothing. I'm preparing for you to stretch me vastly and for you to comfortably eat.

Today my heightened awareness is:

Today's reawakening is:

Today's note to my baby:

Thursday

Cotton seems to be my fashion statement. It's comfortable and allows my body energy to circulate freely. It keeps me warm or cool, whichever I need.

Today my concern is:

Today I acknowledge:

Today's note to my baby:

Come! Tis the red dawn
   of the day,
Maryland!
Come with thy panopolied
   array,
Maryland.
Dear mother, burst the
   tyrant's chain,
Maryland!

James Ryder Randall

Friday

Given conditions
As they be,
Desire no thing
Beyond what is
Now.

Jack Crimmins

I seem to want more and more of my surroundings to be peaceful and serene and harmonious. No need to wait for you to arrive; we'll stroll today in beautiful scenery. A daily mindful walk, being only in the moment. No thoughts of past or future allowed.

Today I want to avoid:

Today I want to address:

Today's note to my baby:

Saturday

Everything I see vibrates within me and has the potential to nourish you. What I focus on visually is as important to you as my food intake. Every day until you're born will be a treasure hunt.

Today's vulnerability is:

Today my purpose is:

Today's note to my baby:

Take my hand,
Together
We can break the lock,
Emerge
Into
Choice,
And live happily ever free.

Helen Whitaker

Sunday

After you arrive, you'll teach me many things. Each moment for you will be a new one filled with all possibilities. Just contemplating you has enlightened me. Each moment for me is new also, but I don't often realize that. Thank you, baby guru.

O child, when things have
learned to wear
Wings once, they must
be fain
To keep them always high
and fair.

Sarah Morgan Bryan Piatt

Today my need is:

Today my intuition is:

Today's note to my baby:

Monday

I'm continuing to nourish us both. Frequent small meals are easier and more comfortable than three large ones. You take up a lot of space.

I'm on the shore and
thou on the sea,
All of thy wanderings
far and near,
Bring thee at last to
shore and me

Bret Harte

Today my resistance is:

Today my aspirations are:

Today's note to my baby:

Tuesday

I know our prenatal vitamins, rich in iron and folic acid, are no substitute for food, but they are important as a supplement. I must remember to take them every day. I am learning about continuity, order, routine, and responsibility—good lessons to learn before you are born.

Somewhere nearby

As inside her

There is a lost spring,

   water, movement

The sustenance of

   canyons

Jack Crimmins

Today my limitations are:

Today my desire is:

Today's note to my baby:

Wednesday

Your daddy has a strong influence on my feelings and emotions. This is a time when we need to encourage and support each other more than usual. There is so much to talk about.

Today my denial is:

Today I am grateful for:

Today's note to my baby:

I am the one who says
  prayer is touch
You are the one
  who says
  touch is prayer
We sing of differences
We are all together here.

Jack Crimmins

Thursday

One day of the woods and
  their balmy light,
One hour on top of a
  breezy hill.

Thomas Wentworth
Higginson

Our intimate connection is still intact. I have begun to think about the change in our relationship after you are born. There is a part of me that wants to hold on to you inside.

Today my heightened awareness is:

Today's reawakening is:

Today's note to my baby:

Friday

I feel a bit anxious about severing our tie when you've reached term. I know it's important for you not to be forever attached to me. After all, this life you are now living inside of me is yours. I am only here to nurture and support you.

Dance upon the shore;
What need have you of care
For wind or water's roar?
And tumble out your hair.

William Butler Yeats

Today my concern is:

Today I acknowledge:

Today's note to my baby:

Saturday

All of my various realizations sometimes border on being overwhelming. Meditation is another important facet of a simple vaginal birth, as is an acceptance of our impending new and different relationship.

Like the song of a bright

yellow canary

This power sings in my

heart.

Helen Whitaker

Today I want to avoid:

Today I want to address:

Today's note to my baby:

Sunday

Today we shall meditate. I will sit in a chair with my feet on the floor a bit apart and my hands open in my lap. I'll close my eyes and will focus on my exhalations for five minutes. That's just the beginning. By the time you're born, we'll be seasoned meditators, you and I. Peaceful floatings.

Today's vulnerability is:

Today my purpose is:

Today's note to my baby:

The mulberry is
a double tree.
Mulberry, shade me,
shade me awhile,
It is a shape of life
described
By another shape
without a word
Mulberry, shade me,
shade me awhile.

Wallace Stevens

Monday

On clear quiet days,

when mind and body

are still,

I sense her presence

within me.

Helen Whitaker

Well, here we are, back in our meditation position. Today we'll do the same as we did yesterday, and then we'll sit for five more minutes actively listening—you to my heartbeat and me to the silence of you within me. Ten minutes of sitting perfectly still. Such luxury.

Today my need is:

Today my intuition is:

Today's note to my baby:

Tuesday

This meditation is really good for my heart rate and my blood pressure. Even my digestion is affected positively. We're off to a deeper state of relaxation. This is a good way to prepare for labor. It's a process where your participation is helpful.

Today my resistance is:

Today my aspirations are:

Today's note to my baby:

I wait until late at night;
When the energy of the city
*   is down*
Most every one is sleeping
Open the window
Even just a little
Listen
To whatever silence
Remains

Jack Crimmins

Wednesday

'Mong the feet of

angels seven

What a dancer,

glimmering!

All the heavens bow down

to Heaven,

Flame to flame and

wing to wing.

William Butler Yeats

When you are ready to be born, I want to be ready to open my cervix and my mind. Today I sit silently for ten minutes and focus again on my exhalations. I automatically inhale, as you will when you take your first breath. Now I shall alternate sending my exhalations down my right and left leg. Concentrating and focusing are important preparations.

Today my limitations are:

Today my desire is:

Today's note to my baby:

Thursday

Today we continue to sit silently together for ten minutes. Pregnancy, labor, and birth are natural. Women have been doing this for ages. "All I have to do is to keep my mind out of my body's way of the work it so well knows how to do"—our new mantra for labor. Now I close my eyes and listen not to my thoughts but to you and to my body.

Today my denial is:

Today I am grateful for:

Today's note to my baby:

And so in mountain
Solitudes—o'ertaken as
by some spell divine—
Their cares dropped from
them like the needles
shaken
From out the gusty pine.

Bret Harte

Friday

It's meditation time again. Today when I close my eyes I shall observe my thoughts. I will not cling to them; I will not judge them; I will not push them away. I shall only observe them. It is a good way of letting go of the unnecessary. Good-bye world. I look forward to my ten minutes of silence.

So sweet to kiss,
so fair to view;
The night comes down,
the lights burn blue
And at my door the pale
horse stands
To bear me forth to
unknown lands

John Hay

Today my heightened awareness is:

Today's reawakening is:

Today's note to my baby:

Saturday

There are subtle energy centers along the center of my body (and yours as well). These energy centers are much like the bond between you and me—they can't be seen or measured. Here's to silence, other ways of knowing, and the resonating harmony we share.

Were we only white birds,

my beloved, buoyed out

in the foam of the sea!

William Butler Yeats

Today my concern is:

Today I acknowledge:

Today's note to my baby:

Sunday

Yet there is still the peace of

ancestors within me.

The gathering of families

takes place in my body

Where the blood

Reunites in my rivers and

streams and joins

within you.

Jack Crimmins

I talked about energy centers yesterday. Knowing where these energy centers are may be of some help during labor. I don't want anything getting clogged. We need a vital flow. There are seven energy centers: one is at the base of my spine (and yours too, of course), and one is below my navel—that's an important one during labor. I'll focus on these two places today, while sending my breath to free the energy that might need unhinging. Off again to ten minutes of silence and focused breathing. I'm getting better at this. It's strange, but it's actually rather fun.

Today I want to avoid:

Today I want to address:

Today's note to my baby:

Monday

A third energy center is right around my navel; if blocked, it can inter-fere with my digestion. Energy center number four is right in the center of my chest, between my two nipples; this is the center from which flows all my love for you. Number five is in my throat; it has to do with communication and creativity. We're doing pretty well in that area. Just to make certain they are functioning as well as possible, in today's meditation I'll focus my exhalations on these three areas. No kicking for ten minutes, please.

Today's vulnerability is:

Today my purpose is:

Today's note to my baby:

I shut my eyes now,
thinking how t'will be
How face to face each soul
Will slip its long control

Nora Perry

Tuesday

Probably there will always
   be things misunderstood
Lost, between us all.
The life the Paiutes lived
   and lost
Is remembered by the one
   who orchestrates winds,
By the root-builder
Who holds up mountains

Jack Crimmins

The sixth energy center is located between my eyebrows (something you just recently grew). This is the place where the yogis focus when they walk on fire so that they feel no pain. I wonder how painful contractions are. On a scale of one to ten, I think they're a ten or maybe even off the scale. If the yogis can do it, I can at least imagine being able to attain a pain scale of three. In today's silence I will focus on the point between my eyebrows.

Today my need is:

Today my intuition is:

Today's note to my baby:

Wednesday

Yesterday's focus is very important, so I'll continue to do that daily. Energy center number seven is located at the top of my head. I think about your magical head and how your bone plates slide together to safely reduce the diameter of your skull as you pass through me on your way out and into my arms. Today I send my breath to protect your crowning soft spot. Your body is so flexible. May your spirit be the same.

Today my resistance is:

Today my aspirations are:

Today's note to my baby:

For the good are always
the merry,
Save by an evil chance,
And the merry love
the fiddle
And the merry love to
dance.

William Butler Yeats

Thursday

Still cheerily the chickadee

Singeth to me on fence

and tree;

But in my inmost ear

is heard

The music of a holier bird

John Townsend Trowbridge

Could it be true that you are wiggling your way downward? I feel a bit more room in my upper abdomen. I can breathe freely again.

Today my limitations are:

Today my desire is:

Today's note to my baby:

Friday

The thought of your descent at once thrills me and makes me a bit anxious. I hope there is room for you as you wend your way through the birth canal. I worry about that sometimes.

Still there's a sense of

blossoms yet unborn

In the sweet airs of morn

Henry Timrod

Today my denial is:

Today I am grateful for:

Today's note to my baby:

Saturday

At times a fragrant breeze
comes floating by,
And brings, you know
not why,
A feeling as when eager
crowds await
Before a palace gate.

Henry Timrod

My lungs are expanding with great joy at each inhalation. I had forgotten how pleasurable a long, deep inhalation can be. May your first breath be as wondrous to you as it will be to me.

Today my heightened awareness is:

Today's reawakening is:

Today's note to my baby:

Sunday

What is it like to breathe for the first time? Is it like inhaling the first scent of spring that arrives on a gentle breeze, or is it like a thrust of a cold winter's gale, harsh and penetrating upon your entire being?

I never saw a moon,
I never saw the sea;
Yet know I how the
   heather looks,
And what a wave must be.

Emily Dickinson

Today my concern is:

Today I acknowledge:

Today's note to my baby:

Monday

One almost looks to see the

very street

Grown purple at his feet.

Henry Timrod

Oh, you are so safe, so protected! I don't care that you are now perched in such a fashion that there is more pressure on my bladder and my rectum. I am getting tired of being pregnant, and yet the thought of you floating inside of me is more soothing than considering your bursting forth into this vast world.

Today I want to avoid:

Today I want to address:

Today's note to my baby:

Tuesday

It's difficult for me to feel comfortable at all now. Lying on my left side gives some relief. What about you? Can you feel my mounting excitement? Do you know it's getting close to your arrival? Are you ready? Actually, this is a delightful place. You won't be cramped any more, yet you'll feel safe. I'll protect you.

Today's vulnerability is:

Today my purpose is:

Today's note to my baby:

Come hither, finding home!

Lo, my new fields of

  harvest, open free

By winds of blessing

  blown.

Whose golden corn blades

  shake from sea to sea.

John Jones Plaitt

Wednesday

Under the joy that is felt

lie the infinite issues

of feeling;

Crowning the glory

revealed, is the

glory that crowns

the revealing.

Richard Realf

I think a lot about my participation in your outbound journey. I promise to make it as short and easy as possible. I shall give you my undivided attention for twenty minutes daily from now on. We shall meditate together and visualize your passage.

Today my need is:

Today my intuition is:

Today's note to my baby:

Thursday

Meditation: I sit comfortably in a chair with my feet on the floor. My hands are on my abdomen, sending caresses to you.

Today my resistance is:

Today my aspirations are:

Today's note to my baby:

Good night! I have to say
good night
To such host of peerless
things!
Good night unto the perfect
mouth,
And all the sweetness
nestled there.

Thomas Bailey Aldrich

Friday

Fine stuff

The well Water

From which true essences

Spring

Jack Crimmins

Meditation: I sit comfortably in a chair with my feet on the floor. My eyes are closed and my breathing is quiet. I listen only to my breath and hope you feel the soothing rhythm as my belly rises and falls.

Today my limitations are:

Today my desire is:

Today's note to my baby:

Saturday

Meditation: I sit comfortably in a chair with my feet flat on the floor. I focus on the area between my two eyebrows. I watch my thoughts parade across my mind. I do not grasp them; I do not force them away. I only focus on the silence inside. We are at one in the calm of my being.

Today my denial is:

Today I am grateful for:

Today's note to my baby:

Open the door of thy heart,
And open thy chamber
*   door*
And my kisses shall teach
*   thy lips*
The love that shall fade
*   no more.*

Bayard Taylor

Sunday

High between dream and
day and think how there
The soul might rise visible
as a flower.

E. J. Scovell

Meditation: I sit as comfortably as I can in a chair with my feet flat on the floor. I focus on the perfection of you, and I send you a healing white light from the center of my two brows to the center of yours. A brilliant white umbilicus of light flowing from me to you and from you to me.

Today my heightened awareness is:

Today's reawakening is:

Today's note to my baby:

Monday

Meditation: Again, I sit as comfortably as possible with my spine straight in my chair and my feet flat on the floor. I repeat to myself, "My body, in its great archetypal wisdom, knows exactly how to give birth to you. All I have to do is to keep my mind out of my body's way of the work it so well knows how to do." I shall repeat this as a mantra to myself whenever I feel the slightest bit anxious.

Today my concern is:

Today I acknowledge:

Today's note to my baby:

*Peach blossoms fallen
on running stream
pass by;
This is an earthly
paradise beneath
the sky.*

Li Bai

Tuesday

Beneath the tree,

inside the gate

Her hair adorned,

she comes to wait.

Anonymous

Meditation: In a chair again. My eyes are closed, my hands are relaxed, my jaw is relaxed. I practice sending every other exhalation deep into my uterus and out through my cervix and my vagina. I hope you are enjoying these deep states of relaxation and alone time together.

Today I want to avoid:

Today I want to address:

Today's note to my baby:

Wednesday

Meditation: Sometimes I wonder if I can birth you vaginally. I really don't want a C-section. I close my eyes, and I visualize you and me at term. I have a lot of tension in my body when I think of birthing you. I increase the tension in my feet, legs, chest, arms, and hands; then I release it. I inhale through my nose and breathe in the healing forces from the universe as my abdomen rises with my breath. I then slowly release my breath through my mouth, sending it deep into my perineum. I focus on the peacefulness of you within me.

Today's vulnerability is:

Today my purpose is:

Today's note to my baby:

The night wind
  of August
Is like an old mother
  to me,
It Comforts me.
I rest in it,
As one would rest,
If one could,
Once again—

Wallace Stevens

Thursday

My steps are nightly
   driven,
By the fever in my heart,
To hear from thy lattice
   breath
The word that shall give
   me rest.

Bayard Taylor

I sit here quieting my anxious mind by focusing on my breath. As I breathe in and breathe out, as I focus on each inhalation and exhalation, I am almost in a trance. This week, you receive your own breath. Your lungs mature, which means that when you are born your respirations will be as easy and as natural as mine are now.

Today my need is:

Today my intuition is:

Today's note to my baby:

Friday

I imagine you here, fresh and new and wet on my abdomen, your breath and my breath rising and falling in unison. One day, we'll go to the headlands high above the ocean; the seagulls will soar and ride the wind, while you and I fill our lungs with the clear air. We'll laugh and shout with glee as we breathe without a thought and look together at the myriad colors of the wildflowers and the sky. Develop, little lungs, make yourselves complete! It's not long before your first respiration.

Today my resistance is:

Today my aspirations are:

Today's note to my baby:

The sails, like flakes of roseate pearl,
Float in upon the mist;
The waves are broken precious stones,
Sapphire and amethyst.

Lucy Larcom

Saturday

Mother and child,

    lover and lover mated,

Are wound and bound

    together and enflowing

What has been plaited

    cannot be unplaited.

          May Sarton

Stay within a bit longer. Reap more of the benefits from your uterine hideaway. Gather all the immunities that you can. Eat and drink of me. Sup to your heart's delight. Stay here until you've reached term. It's the best place for you now.

Today my limitations are:

Today my desire is:

Today's note to my baby:

Sunday

My abdomen is grand with the size of you. I want you to stay, yet I'm feeling uncomfortable. I sit here again in silence. I send my thoughts out to sea. I let go of my fear and tension. I breathe in the serenity of a vast, blue sky and I send that calm throughout my body. I float on the fluffy cumulus clouds, and my body feels free and weightless. I am at peace as we journey together, abandoning ourselves in silence.

Today my denial is:

Today I am grateful for:

Today's note to my baby:

*Such a beautiful pail of
fish, such a beautiful
peck of apples,
I cannot bring you now
It is too early and I am not
footloose yet.*

Carl Sandburg

Monday

I've heard talk that formula is healthier and easier than breast-feeding. I still have some reservations about the process of nursing you. The way I see it, my milk is ready to flow for you. It would be a shame to deprive you of that wonderful bond that we can continue to develop. Its temperature is perfect for you. It has all the nutrients you need. You are less likely to get sick if I suckle you. When I think of all the chores of life I must deal with after you are born, I can't think of any more delightful respite than to sit with you as a life force from my breast trickles into your eager mouth.

Today my heightened awareness is:

Today's reawakening is:

Today's note to my baby:

Tuesday

I still wonder about breast-feeding. One advantage is its availability and convenience. I don't have to prepare it, I don't have to shop for it, and it's one less expense. I do have a practical side—I'm not just a pregnant romantic. Again I contemplate relaxing and feeding you. I shall make the time to nurse you for at least three to six months. It's also good for my uterus. Nursing you reduces the risk of hemorrhage and causes my uterus to return to its normal size quickly and naturally. That's certainly a plus. Yet, I'm still not certain.

Today my concern is:

Today I acknowledge:

Today's note to my baby:

Sunshine of late

afternoon—

On the glass tray.

William Carlos Williams

Wednesday

There are still some who are trying to convince me to bottle-feed you. If I breast-feed you, you will have a much smaller chance of having upper respiratory infections, ear infections, and colon infections. You'll be less likely to have allergies, and you'll be calmer. All of this also means that I'll have more time to do what I need and want to do. If I feel anxious or uncomfortable or feel as though I don't know what I'm doing, I'll ask for help. If at the last minute I decide to bottle-feed you, at least I know that I will have done the best that I can do.

Today I want to avoid:

Today I want to address:

Today's note to my baby:

Thursday

When you arrive, I shall massage you with sesame oil. Until then, I'll pay special attention to you through my enormous belly. Every time I touch my abdomen, you seem to answer with a gesture: your first game.

Today I'm going to purchase scented oils to massage my body, especially my breasts, in preparation for you. The sesame oil is great, but I need some variety now. I think I will try a mixture of 4 tablespoons sweet almond oil, 1 tablespoon avocado oil, 10 drops tangerine oil, and 5 drops lavender oil.

Today's vulnerability is:

Today my purpose is:

Today's note to my baby:

After dressing my hair,
Alone I climb the stair
On the railings I lean
To view the river scene,
A thousand sails pass by
But not the one for which
  wait I.

Wen Tingyun

Friday

Come, you are to lose your

freshness.

Will you drift into the net

willingly.

Dylan Thomas

Labor meditation: You are still growing, and I'm curious as to how you will manage to squeeze through your birthing passage. I send to you a white light of love and lubrication. I imagine you, at term, being guided down through my body on this path of light, surrounded by it and filled with it. The same light softens, ripens, and easily dilates my cervix and pushes you out into the baby catcher's hands. It is with great ease that we perform this miracle.

Today my need is:

Today my intuition is:

Today's note to my baby:

Saturday

Tonight before sleep, I'll take a warm bath—a practice first-stage-of-labor bath. I'll add two to three drops of lavender oil to the water, then I'll relax, soak, empty my mind, and focus on the rise and fall of my abdomen for ten minutes. I'll climb into bed totally relaxed, and I'll sleep peacefully. Sometimes I get a bit frightened and I'm not sure why. If I stay in the now, I feel safe. I trust my relaxed body.

Today my resistance is:

Today my aspirations are:

Today's note to my baby:

*They halted at
   a terrace wall;
Below, the towered city lay;
The valley in the moonlight
   thrall
Was silent in a swoon
   of May.*

Robert Underwood Johnson

Sunday

Days and months appear
long in the fairyland
halls.

Bai Ju-Yi

I plan on relaxing with you daily this week. Soon our labor will begin. I know whatever I think and feel and hear affects you. I know whatever drugs I take during labor will also affect you. I'll do my best to give you a drug-free beginning. I want to have an alternative to drugs.

Today my limitations are:

Today my desire is:

Today's note to my baby:

Monday

I wonder if you somehow sense that you will soon be moving from your warm and dark fluid habitat to a very bright and spacious world. I'm feeling all sorts of different physical sensations, which I'm certain you must be experiencing also. You don't have very much space in there anymore.

Dost thou dream of what
was and no more is;
The old kingdom of earth
and the kings?

Algernon Charles Swinburne

Today my denial is:

Today I am grateful for:

Today's note to my baby:

Tuesday

I shall prepare us nutritionally for this labor. I need to eat several small meals a day, as there seems to be very little room for anything more. Oatmeal, cottage cheese, nuts, seeds, lots of plain yogurt, vegetables, egg whites, and some apples—simple, nourishing, and fresh, similar to a marathon runner's diet. I feel excited, a little impatient, and somewhat uncertain.

Today my heightened awareness is:

Today's reawakening is:

Today's note to my baby:

Wednesday

I imagine the contractions of labor having a wave-like feeling, rising to a crest and then gently rolling into shore and subsiding until the next contraction. I close my eyes and see myself and imagine a gradual tightening and then a gripping of the muscles in my lower abdomen or in the small of my back. I see myself both riding a grand wave and being that wave at the same time. As the wave spreads and rises and tilts my uterus forward, you are pressed down closer and closer to your first breath.

Today my concern is:

Today I acknowledge:

Today's note to my baby:

Purity pleases heaven:
all must wear clean
garments
And purify their hands
with running water.

Albius Tibullus

Thursday

I will gather flowers my
  Corydon
To set in thy cap.

Anonymous

I visualize each swell of my belly and each rise of my uterus as a magnificent and incredibly powerful force, wild and rhythmical as the great thrusts of the ocean. I see you being moved down the aisle of an ancient cathedral in a divine moment of silence. No organ could resound the emergent energy of your new life. With each contraction, you move downward and outward; I then relax in abeyance to your force. So we shall proceed, you and I, until I hold you in my arms.

Today I want to avoid:

Today I want to address:

Today's note to my baby:

Friday

Here I am, contemplating you again. When the first stage of labor arrives, if my bag of waters has not broken, I shall soak again in a warm bath with some lavender oil. I hear this will help my uterus to contract more efficiently and will reduce the pressure I feel from inside of me. I wonder what labor is like for you. I like thinking that the rise and fall of my uterus gently massages you as it bids you farewell.

The rising sun appears sublime
But O! Tis near your birthing time.

Anonymous

Today's vulnerability is:

Today my purpose is:

Today's note to my baby:

Saturday

Ah! When will this long

weary day have end,

And lende me leave to come

unto my love?

How slowly do the houres

theyr numbers spend!

Edmund Spenser

Today I send you an invitation. You have been a most welcome resident, although I hope that you don't stay inside for too much longer. Outside, the sun shines, the flowers blossom and toss scents of pleasure in the air, the clouds play tag, and the butterflies do the same. Rain falls and rivers flow, trees grow high in the sky, vegetables grow from the earth; gentle breezes will kiss your face, and stems of nipples with streams of milk are waiting for your wanting mouth. Last, but not least, I cannot possibly grow another inch. Do come soon. Love, Mommy.

Today my need is:

Today my intuition is:

Today's note to my baby:

Sunday

I shall not sit and wait for you. I'll go to the garden or to the park. I'll walk and admire other creations. I'll listen to music and do anything I can to keep my mind out of my body's way. I am ready for your entrance. Please come. Are you really still comfortable in there? I don't want to force you out, but at this point I think it's healthier for the two of us, both physically and emotionally, if you come into my arms. I'm tired and stretched; I'm uncomfortable and a bit impatient.

Today my resistance is:

Today my aspirations are:

Today's note to my baby:

So waste not thou; but
  come for all the vales
Await thee; azure pillows
  of the hearth
Arise to thee; the children
  call, and I
Thy shepherd pipe, and
  sweet is every sound
Sweeter thy voice, but
  every sound is sweet;
Myriads of rivulets
  hurrying thro' the lawn,
The moan of doves in
  immemorial elms
And murmuring of
  innumerable bees.

Alfred Tennyson

Monday

Last night, i pulled the

moon down

out of the sky and onto my

waiting belly.

Ruth Lerner

There are molecules that regulate the production of progesterone in your fetal membranes, in my placenta, in the lining of my uterus, and in the muscle cells of my uterus. We are a team, you and I, a unique collaborative system.

Today my limitations are:

Today my desire is:

Today's note to my baby:

Tuesday

When the prostaglandin regulating molecules inhibit the progesterone production, the process of birth begins. I visualize the progesterone decreasing and the prostaglandin increasing.

Come with us and you'll collect
Golden suns around your neck!

Jules La Forgue

Today my denial is:

Today I am grateful for:

Today's note to my baby:

Wednesday

I visualize the molecules as friendly and competent. They aid my cervix in softening and dilating. Let the process of birthing begin!

Today my heightened awareness is:

Today's reawakening is:

Today's note to my baby:

Thursday

I hope that my pituitary gland soon secretes oxytocin, a hormone that is another factor in the contraction of my uterus.

Each brightening day
Adds honey to its store.

Paul Valéry

Today my concern is:

Today I acknowledge:

Today's note to my baby:

Friday

The sky! Give up!

   Come to the ball

And you will turn the

   heads of all

Our very most

   distinguished stars.

Jules La Forgue

I visualize all of the secretions effectively causing the muscles of your uterine home to contract. With incredible momentum birthing begins and proceeds until you and your placenta have arrived. Please come out easily.

Today I want to avoid:

Today I want to address:

Today's note to my baby:

Saturday

Come my wonderful child, let my uterus squeeze you down the birth canal. I imagine my contractions as coordinated and efficient. Enjoy the full massage as your head and body easily move through the gentle stimulation of your first passage. I realize that you begin the process of birth and that I must be ready in order to complete it. I am ready. I await you.

Patience; patience
Patience in the Blueness!
Every atom of silence
Is a seed of ripeness
The glad surprise will
  come.

Paul Valéry

Today's vulerability:

Today my purpose is:

Today's note to my baby:

Things to Take to the Birthing Room

Cotton clothes for me to wear

Cotton socks

Tape deck

Leclaire labor and music tape

Warm miso soup in a thermos for me to sip in early labor

Rolling pin in case of back labor

Lavender oil to smell

Something beautiful to look at

Recollections of . . .

My labor:

Your birth:

Your first hour of life:

Baby Facts

Your name:

Your weight:

Your height:

Hour of birth:

Day of birth:

Place of birth:

Other people present during your birth:

Creative Childbirth: The Complete Leclaire Method
(Book, 104 pages)
$11.95

Tape I
Side A: *Hypnosis and Pregnancy*
Side B: *Relaxation Sounds—Dawn at Coral Canyon Beach*
$9.95

Tape II
Side A: *Hypnosis for Labor (to be played during thirty-ninth week and as soon as you go into the first stage of labor and throughout labor as needed)*
Side B: *Relaxation Sounds—Sunset at Coral Canyon Beach*
$9.95

The Work Book *includes exercises on how to gain emotional mastery and comfort regarding your beliefs about pregnancy, labor, birthing, and motherhood.*
$6.95

Music tape

Side A and B: Baroque Music

Largo movements for centering the right and left brain. For relaxation, concentration, and meditation during pregnancy; labor; birthing; breast feeding; and sleepless nights.

$13.95

Meditation and Healing Tape

For nausea, herpes, stress, cancer, and HIV.

$9.95

Full Leclaire Package

$49.95

For all orders, please include a flat rate of $4.00 for shipping and handling and send a check or money order only. California residents please add sales tax. Products will be sent via U.S. Priority Mail.

For further information or to order, please write or call:

Michelle Leclaire O'Neill, Ph.D., R.N.

P.O. Box 1086

Pacific Palisades, CA 90272

(310) 454-0920